Here Be (Rude) Dragons!

General Warning:

This book *does* contain some naughty words. It's *mainly* bad poetry, a few naïve opinions and a smattering of wishy-washy idealistic nonsense, but a little swearing did creep in, despite absolutely no effort at all to prevent it.

If you like poetry you'll probably find my attempts at rhyming and scansion far more offensive than the occasional profanity, but you have now been warned, so proceed at your own effing peril.

Audio Version Warning:

If you are listening to the audio version of this book then some extra warnings are necessary; firstly visual homophonic word plays (i.e. puns) do *not* always translate well to audio format, and secondly, and probably more worryingly, not only do I recite the poems, but I also try to "sing" the songs.

I can only hope that any physical injury or mental distress this causes is neither too severe nor lasting[1].

---

[1] Does NOT constitute an admission of legal liability.

Four Words

This book is rubbish.

Forewords

By justageezer

Herein, gentle reader, you will find a collection of short poems, rhymes and the odd song or two originally posted by myself in the comments sections of various Ars Technica articles.

A few have been slightly edited and tidied up since their original publication; they're not much better now, but at least I don't think there are any typos. There *is* a mix of Ars' American and my British English, but anything that looks like a typo is actually clever artistic expression, OK?

I would be the first to admit that the quality varies; some stand out as being not very good, and I hope you'll enjoy those, as the rest are all worse. In my defence I can only say that they were mostly written in a matter of minutes, so I could post them near the top of the comment threads, and thus ~~annoy~~ amuse as many people as possible. Also I suck at poetry.

Covering an eclectic range of topics, there really is something here for almost everyone to dislike, and as they span a period from 2012 – 2024 some of the older, more topical ones may now make little or no sense. So, no change really.

By Ars Technica (probably)

Who? Oh, *that* guy. We'd like to get rid of him, but he hasn't actually broken any rules. Yet.

Preface – A Myopic Synopsis

Imagine putting Albert Einstein and Stephen Hawking, Elvis Presley and John Denver, John Keats and William Shakespeare, and Elon Musk and Mark Zuckerberg into a very large mincer – and mincing them. Yuck, right?

Then imagine a very large, hungry pig eats that mince, and consequently produces a huge, steaming turd. This book is that turd. Only *smaller*. Please wash your hands after reading.

Table of Contents

NATURE...15
Synthetic jellyfish a hybrid of rat hearts and plastic...............15
Employment Enjoyment..16
Organism without a brain creates external memories for navigation...17
George's Great Escape..18
Virus turns bacteria's defenses against them............................20
War. War Never Changes..20
New phylum of bacteria found lurking in hospital sink's drain. 22
A Film Review..23
Molecular signals identified that let some organisms regrow lost heads...24
Worm, Whole!..25
Projected climate change moves much faster than land vertebrates have evolved..26
Many Cells Good, One Cell Better...27
Do bees know what they don't know?.......................................28
To Bee..28
Santa's revenge: Arctic ice may be putting US in a long, deep freeze...29
Leaving, On A Jet Ski...30
More evidence that microbes inhabit lakes deep under Antarctic ice..31
Decimation by Observation..32
Common food emulsifiers may be linked to metabolic syndrome...33
Consider Your Lining When Dining..34
Drones used to monitor bears send their heart rates through

the roof	35
Not Their Necessities	36
New analysis confirms hypothesis for source of mysterious auroral "dunes"	37
Galileo and Juliet	38
It's time to fear the fungi	39
Who Foretold The Mould?	40
Over 100 different species made this 2,200-year-old shipwreck home, study finds	41
No Finer Diner	42
COVID-infected hamsters in pet shop trigger animal cull in Hong Kong	43
Worstiality	43
We now know how cats purr—why they purr is still up for debate	44
I Purr Because	45
Where the heck did all those structures inside complex cells come from?	46
Look Inside	47
Tracking the genes that turn a fungus into a carnivore	48
Delicious Binds	49
Getting to the bottom of how red flour beetles absorb water through their butts	50
Defecation Desiccation	51
Rare bubonic plague case in Oregon spread from very sick pet cat	52
Even Worstiality	52
Variant of a toad-based psychedelic can act as an antidepressant	53
Mr Toad Takes A Trip	54
The wasps that tamed viruses	55
Viral Infection By Larval Injection	56

Whale songs have features of language, but whales may not

be speaking...57
A Song of Ice and Mire......................................58
SCIENCE...**59**
Meteorites, not comets, may have brought water to Earth.. 59
Nicer Ice... 60
The fruits of string theory: The Shape of Inner Space............ 61
The String's The Thing..61
Can non-Newtonian fluid behaviour explain stuck ketchup bottles?... 62
Messing With Dressing... 62
Heavy ion collisions reveal the earliest instants of our Universe... 63
The Theoretical Physicist of Venice............................ 64
Researchers control reactions between just two atoms........ 65
Hyperfine State of Mind...66
Disentangling photons and atoms to keep quantum systems clean...67
Here's Johnny!..68
New type of quantum excitation behaves like a solitary particle... 69
A Simple Sentence...69
Is the lopsided Universe telling us we need new theories?.. 70
Asymmetricality We Love Thee................................... 71
Is entanglement real or is there a super-deterministic cosmic conspiracy?...72
Quasars Set To Stun.. 73
Graphene allows strange form of ice to occur at room temperature... 74
Even Nicer Ice..74
Tiny diamonds wrapped in graphene get rid of friction.........75

Grapholene!	76
Archaeologists find evidence of neurons in glassy brain of Vesuvius victim	77
Frozen In Thought	78
Researchers cool a 40 kg object to near its quantum ground state	79
Reflection Perfection	80
Brrr	80
What fractals, Fibonacci, and the golden ratio have to do with cauliflower	81
Harmonic Mnemonic	82
Marsquakes illuminate what lies beneath the sands of Mars	83
Celestial Fruit	84
European project sets a record for fusion energy produced by a tokamak	85
Full Nuclear Ahead to the Steam Age	86
The coolest instrument in space: Building the Webb's MIRI	87
On First Looking Into The Mid-Infrared	88
The snow forecast for Mars: Dry ice and a meter a year	89
And Now The Weather	90
Remains of planet that formed the Moon may be hiding near Earth's core	91
Lunar Tessera Interred in Terra	92
Daily Telescope: Black holes have been merging for a long, long time	93
To Be Hole	93
TECH	**94**
NASA partners with Microsoft to launch its first launch video game	94
Lander Plunder	95
Meet Yeti, the South Pole's crevasse-detecting robot	96

Cracking Tracking, Tracking Cracking / (Smallfoot) 98
Kim Dotcom's answer to Spotify and iTunes – Baboom – will soft launch on Monday 99
Dotcom Begone 101
Taylor Swift wages a campaign against ad-supported music streaming 102
The Last Swift of Autumn 104
Gallery: we tear apart a $340 audiophile Ethernet cable and look inside 106
The Emperor's New Cables 107
Facebook's metaverse gambit is a distraction from its deep-seated problems 108
The Betterverse 109
President Biden to host infosec roundtable with tech giant CEOs 110
Slomo Joe 111
Apple fixes security vulnerabilities in new versions of iOS, macOS, and watchOS 112
iFail 113
At the age of 90, Captain f'n Kirk is finally going to space today 114
To Boldly Go 115
Getting software to "hallucinate" reasonable protein structures 116
Groot's Roots? 117
Jurassic-period ammonite fossils flex their muscles in virtual 3D 118
Ammonite Acolyte 119
Game dev group says addressing NFT gaming's "ethical issues" is a "priority" 120
Blockchain Gravy Train 121

Elon Musk would let Trump back on Twitter, says ban was "morally wrong"	122
Muskrat Rap	123
Meta highlights NFT, blockchain hopes as it shutters its Novi crypto wallet	124
Crypto Through the Tulips	125
Double-screen "free" TV will show you ads, even when not in use	126
TV This Century	126
Patreon attacks law that keeps platforms from sharing your video views	127
The Meta Pixel	128
Game dev says contract barring "subjective negative reviews" was a mistake	129
Play – Nice	130
Twitter URLs redirect to x.com as Musk gets closer to killing the Twitter name	131
Twiticide	132

SOCIAL ... 133

Did Prenda try to intimidate ID theft victim into dropping charges?	133
The Legend of Prenda	135
"I made some stupid posts": Anti-troll site gagged after threats against poet	136
The Rash	137
Random access memories: My time at a singularity conference	138
Buying Time	139
Texas school board approves all but one science text book	140
The Devil Went Down To Texas	141
"Happy Birthday" copyright defense: Those "words" and "text" are ours	143

Totally Not "Happy Birthday"......144
Science confirms: Online trolls are horrible people (also, sadists!)......145
Trolling, Trolling, Trolling......146
Is your smartphone making you dumb?......148
Ode To CorSiritana......149
UK peer calls for universal Internet delete button; may also want unicorns......150
Logan's Hell......151
Cancer patients call for UK government to override patent on £90,000-a-year drug......153
Health. Care?......154
President-elect Biden plans COVID response—while White House faces new outbreak......155
45......156
A $26-billion plan to save the Houston area from rising seas... 157
Galvestunned......158
Is the "Dragon Man" skull actually from a new hominin species?......159
Speciation By Corporation......160
Twitter admits it mistakenly removed Ukraine open-source intelligence accounts......161
Mooting......162
Russia pulls out of European spaceport, abandoning a planned launch......163
Off Topic......164
Majority of Ukrainian hospitals could run out of oxygen today as omicron rages: WHO......165
So Said The Crow......166
Ex-Goop exec decries "toxic" wellness culture—while

promoting a cleanse...167
Excellent Excrement..168
Is the NFL making progress in tackling its concussion crisis?....169
Third And Ten...170
Great British Bake Off's festive Christmas desserts aren't so naughty after all..171
G.B.B.O G.O.O.D..172
MISC..173
The Internet's most hated man..173
Irksome Jerks..174
Limerweek in review: the week's top news in rhyme............175
Poetry Isn't Easy...176
Introducing comment voting on news articles and features 177
Hating Comment Rating...177
Welcome to Ars Technica UK!...179
Ars Britannia..180
LG ad subverting "dark on light" format for home page.........181
Condé Nasty..182
A Neanderthal carved a geometric design in bone 51,000 years ago..183
Neolithic Prick..184
World Brain: Wells, Welles, Orwell, and the role of information in society...185
The Human Lament
(I Don't Believe in Adam and Eve)..187
A look back at (very bad) predictions of global cooling.........189
Cringeworthy..190
Court rules Florida-based cruise lines can ask for vaccine certification..191
The Ballad of Redneck Joe...192
Florida is ablaze with COVID-19—and its case data reporting

is a hot mess..196
The UK CoronaVirus Blues... 197
The 20 most-read stories of 2021 on Ars Technica..............202
Arscape (Not The Pina Coladas Song).......................................202
Animals vs. humans vs. machines: who's got smarts?......... 205
Clever /= Wise...206
Ars Technica content is now available in OpenAI services. 207
Web of Lies...208
Closing Thoughts.. **209**
Dedication...**210**

Dear reader,

Now that you've skipped over that tedious Table of Contents, because this book will probably be found listed alongside proper poetry books, my ego sadly requires me to engage in yet more pre-emptive expectation management.

A compilation of vaguely rhyming comments posted in response to randomly chosen science articles on the Internet has several important differences to a "poetry book", which I'd ask readers to take into account when forming an opinion of this work.

Most, if not all of the poems in most poetry books will be on subjects chosen by the poet, presumably subjects that they feel sufficiently knowledgeable about to describe in verse, and the author can take as long as they feel necessary to produce work of a quality that they are happy to publish.

In this book the rhymes are on subjects chosen by whatever article happened to inspire me, often something with which I had only the most fleeting familiarity, and almost all were written within a self-imposed time limit of five to ten minutes.

Given those parameters I am happy to stand by my work – self-evidently it was the best I could do at the time. In fact, this might actually be *the best* compilation of bad poetry originally posted as article comments on a science website *in the world*!

That's probably just wishful thinking on my part though – if I claim any talent, it is that I'm not too proud to actually put the rubbish I produce into the public domain, in the hope that it might make at least one person smile.

Hopefully that's you.

Finally, should you visit Ars Technica online (which I thoroughly recommend), and find that some of the article headings are different to those in this book, it's not actually an error on my part for once, that's just how Ars works, with A and B headlines for all stories.

Now on to the book ...

NATURE

JOHN TIMMER, JUL 23, 2012

Synthetic jellyfish a hybrid of rat hearts and plastic

This article, reporting on a paper in Nature Biotechnology, relates how researchers at two popular American universities collaborated to create an artificial construct that could swim like a jellyfish.

Jellyfish, specifically *Aurelia Aurita*, produce their swimming motion when a single layer of cells inside their bell contracts and then relaxes. Fortunately for the scientists, cardiac cells, when grown in a culture, will form a single layer that will respond to electrical stimuli by contracting.

By growing a layer of these cells on a lobed, flexible plastic disc, immersing the disc in fluid of the right viscosity and applying an electrical current across the tank, the researchers were able to make their construct swim with efficiency comparable to the real thing.

To me this sounded like a great way to spend your time, though one previously covered by at least one gothic horror novel, as my comment noted.

Employment Enjoyment

A few people have cushy jobs,
(I surely wish I did).
The Harvard / Caltech student mob
Have made a Robo-squid!

(Thinks to myself: This can't be hard,
A modern witches brew:
Heart of rat on Barclaycard –
Yup, think that'll do).

Now add a bit of Frankenstein:
"Wait for the strike, Igor!"
"And when the lightning hits the line
This thing will swim for sure!"

JOHN TIMMER, OCT 8, 2012

Organism without a brain creates external memories for navigation

The fascinating slime mould has been the subject of much scientific study, and this article reports how researchers have discovered how the simple organism, that lacks a brain or nervous system, manages to create a record of where it has been.

Now as the only thing the slime mould can possibly use for this purpose is slime, the conclusions of the paper weren't actually that revelatory; the mould sends out feelers searching for food, unsuccessful feelers are withdrawn leaving behind a trail of slime, and new feelers will not cross these slime paths to avoid duplicating failed searches.

In effect the organism creates an external memory in its environment, similar in some ways to how ants leave pheromone trails to mark routes to food sources, only in the case of the mould it is marking areas where food *wasn't* found.

I tend to feel a little sorry for those species of animals that humans cultivate purely to study, and thought I'd write a comment that turned the tables around for a change.

George's Great Escape

There is a story I've been told
(bear with me, this may take some time),
About a questing blob of slime,
and a scientist that was too bold.

The scientist had captured him,
Ignoring all his natural rights,
And now he spent his days and nights
Completing tasks at master's whim.

A bid for freedom was his wish:
To leave his current cell behind,
And by exploring hope to find
A way to leave his petri dish.

He would not simply serve his time,
Accepting food from master's hand,
But set out to explore the land,
Mapping the confines with his slime.

The master studied him with glee,
Thinking the while he was the best,
And not the subject of the test,
As was the *true* reality.

George (the slime mould), did his job;
Now finished with his clever maps,
He analysed the master's traps,
With condescension – from a blob.

He'd got a single cell outside,
A filament that breached the rim,
Without his master seeing him,
And now he could not be denied!

The scientist was later found
(by his colleague from next door);
He was a puddle on the floor,
with slimy feelers all around.

The moral is, we think we're smart,
even as we play the fool,
And watch those that divide and rule,
They've been here since the very start.

DIANA GITIG, MAR 13, 2013

Virus turns bacteria's defenses against them

Reporting on a story in the journal Nature, this article brings us more details on the processes that bacteria use to avoid infection by viruses – and the countermeasures that viruses have developed to avoid these mechanisms.

When a bacteria defeats an attacking virus it stores part of the attacker's DNA in its own DNA, and if a similar attack is detected in the future it then produces matching RNA that somehow repels the attacker.

Some viral phages, such as the ICP1 phage that attacks Cholera bacteria and was isolated from a Cholera patients diarrhoea, have however developed a counter to this, with their own system of recorded DNA fragments that can activate to destroy the bacteria's version – and can evolve to stay effective despite changes to its target's defences.

The astonishing complexity of what we consider the "simplest" life forms has long fascinated me, and this article inspired another poem coloured by this interest.

War. War Never Changes.

In a bygone age we set the stage for superbug mutations,
We pit our brains against those strains
with 20 minute generations.

'Cos we saved some dead with mouldy bread
and surgeries enhanced,
We have the sense that intelligence
makes *us* the more advanced.
But now's the part where we're not so smart
and realise our deepest fears,
We've met our match; our current catch
has been here four billion years.
They've fought for life through greater strife
than humans can realise,
(And for what it's worth terraformed Earth
from Hell to Paradise).
They'll make their home where we can't roam
in the air or earth or sea,
They evolved a race to take 'em to space,
a member of which is me!

On topic now; we're learning how
these superbeings deal,
With the viral horde; a DNA record –
now this shit just got real.

JOHN TIMMER, JUN 11, 2013

New phylum of bacteria found lurking in hospital sink's drain

Thanks to advances in affordable gene sequencing, researchers, reporting in an article in PNAS, have discovered what they believe is a new phylum of bacteria that is unlike anything previously discovered. Named TM6 this new life form was discovered in a biofilm found in a hospital sink.

With almost half of its genes encoding never seen before proteins, and seemingly lacking some of the cellular machinery required for independent life, it has been proposed that the organism is symbiotic, possibly living inside a eukaryote such as an amoeba.

Using only my natural talents I managed to reduce this rather involved article on advanced biology to something a little less high-brow.

A Film Review

Have you seen the latest biofilm? I think it's pretty hot.
It's got some cool new characters
(though it lacks a bit in plot).

The lead's a chap who always knew he'd make it in the flix,
Despite his parents calling him the catchy 'TM6'.

Now some debate regarding whether he's properly alive;
You'd have to check his brothers first;
that's TMs one through five.

Apparently George Lucas thinks his screen name
should be Darth,
Because he's from the dark side – the dark side of your bath.

From waste pipes and obscurity to a quarter-hour of fame,
A bit-part in evolution is a lead role in a drain.

JOHN TIMMER, JUL 24, 2013

Molecular signals identified that let some organisms regrow lost heads

Planarian worms may not be everyone's idea of an interesting creature, however when it comes to recovering from serious injury some of them have an ability that many *would* find interesting – the ability to regrow missing body parts.

This includes not just regrowing lost tails, but also lost heads and even complete sides. Cut some Planarians in half sideways *or* longways and you get *two* complete Planarians. Some members of the species however lack all or part of this desirable ability, and by studying the differences between the ones that can and the ones that can't scientists, reporting in an article in the journal Nature, have discovered details of the chemical signalling that affects regeneration.

This did involve some direct experimentation, resulting in worms with two heads or two tails. While I appreciate the advances in scientific knowledge I can't help feeling a little sorry for the poor worms, and I thought that my comment could try and show another side of these interesting creatures. Pun, as always, intended.

Worm, Whole!

A warning to the squeamish: this tale may make you squirm,
As a scientist plays Fruit Ninja – only with a tiny worm.

He sliced it and he diced it, for he was a little bored,
(And to act out manly fantasies, with his little ninja sword).

But Wilberforce the worm-like one just took this in his stride,
He grew a front, he grew a back, he grew a new left side.

The scientist was soon found dead
with worms covering his face;
Just another victory for the Planarian master race.

SCOTT K. JOHNSON, JUL 28, 2013

Projected climate change moves much faster than land vertebrates have evolved

According to a paper published in Ecology Letters, researchers set out to answer the question of whether species could evolve to adapt to the projected regional changes being caused by climate change. They did this by studying many closely related pairs of creatures from across the animal kingdom, and working out how quickly they had diverged from each other to fit into different environmental niches.

Their findings probably won't come as a surprise; evolution occurs for "advanced" creatures at rates measured in millennia or millions of years, while climate change is occurring at rates measured in decades or centuries. As such, unless complex life learns how to evolve orders of magnitude faster than previously, its only chance of survival will require moving up, either to higher altitudes or higher latitudes.

I felt beholden to point out that, while our greed and stupidity might cause the extinction of even more species, possibly even including our own, mass extinctions have happened before and will happen again, but the ultimate life form on this planet will survive, so look on the bright side!

Many Cells Good, One Cell Better

We like to think a brain is great; our problems will be solved,
Some even think we are created instead of being evolved,
Above, beyond, better than – best!
Humanity superior to the rest!
And say this with a face that's straight, and no hubris involved.

I'm sorry that I disagree; a long lifespan is fine,
For periods of stability in geologic time,
But change will come, too quick for some,
At which point their duration's done –
Their branch on life's great tree removed from the design.

Yet fear ye not, but feel elation, our masters will survive,
A 20 minute generation ensures they'll stay alive,
So now, while my home brew ferments,
I'll thank those hydro-thermal vents,
For their single-celled creation – from which we all derive.

KATE SHAW YOSHIDA, NOV 5, 2013

Do bees know what they don't know?

This article describes how, in order to study the meta-cognitive abilities of bees, specifically self-awareness of uncertainty, two researchers in Australia created a rather cunning experiment involving two separate potential sources of nourishment.

One provided a tasty treat, the other an unpleasant alternative. Test bees quickly learned which was which, but when the two were moved so that the bees no longer knew where the goodies were the bees usually chose not to choose, instead opting out of the decision and leaving without making a choice.

The idea of an insect that is aware of its own uncertainty could inspire a variety of interesting stories, unfortunately the best I could manage was a silly line of off-topic word play.

To Bee

I knew bees aren't newbies but these new bees are doobies, this news be the bee's knees like Nubian rubies.

JOHN TIMMER, FEB 17, 2014

Santa's revenge: Arctic ice may be putting US in a long, deep freeze

At the time of this article's publication several parts of the northern hemisphere were suffering from unusual winter weather, with freezing temperatures in the US, warm weather in Scandinavia and flooding in the UK.

Much of the weather in these areas is governed by the Jet Stream, fast moving high altitude winds caused by the temperature gradient between the freezing Arctic and the warmer lower latitudes.

These winds circle the North Pole in what is called the Polar Vortex, carrying weather systems around the globe as they do so. Unfortunately as the poles are warming much faster than the lower climes the gradient that causes the Jet Stream is now less steep and more variable, allowing it to wander.

For some reason an old tune by John Denver came to mind while reading this article, as *hopefully* demonstrated by my comment.

Leaving, On A Jet Ski

All my bags are packed, I'm loading the boat,
I'm hoping the damn thing will stay afloat,
I hate to wake you up to see this mess.
But the door is breaking, it's falling down.
And now the water is coming around,
Already it's a state, I must confess.

So kiss me – and bail for me,
Tell me that you're good at sea,
Hold on tight, soon we'll be in Bordeaux,
'Cos we're flooding – blame the jet stream,
Downtown will soon be found downstream,
Oh babe, how I hate this flow ...

With thanks to Mr Denver, from a wet UK.

CYNAN ELLIS-EVANS, AUG 20, 2014

More evidence that microbes inhabit lakes deep under Antarctic ice

The earliest life on Earth survived on inorganic sources of nourishment, and there are still some extreme environments where this type of life continues to flourish, as evidenced by recent results from an experimental foray beneath the Antarctic ice.

By using carefully prepared sterile drilling equipment researchers were able to gather samples from a lake hidden beneath 800m of ice. These revealed a complex ecosystem in this seemingly hostile environment, where there is high pressure, no light, freezing temperatures and little organic matter.

Representatives of both bacteria and archaea were found, however the most common life forms were microbes that could digest inorganic elements, particularly nitrogen in the form of ammonia.

I find these results fascinating if not surprising; an empty dead lake would have been difficult to explain given what we know about how persistent life is, but I did ponder on the effect this research might have on the innocent microbes that were discovered.

Decimation by Observation

In the depths of a sub-glacial sea
There is life – and serenity.
If you could go diving
You'd find life is thriving
On a diet of raw NH_3.

Nothing there ever gets sick,
And death there never comes quick;
(Well, till some died of fright
When exposed to the light
When a scientist took the first pic).

DIANA GITIG, FEB 27, 2015

Common food emulsifiers may be linked to metabolic syndrome

Human intestines are full of bacteria, most of which are not just handy, but actually required for us to extract nutrition from our food. Over recent years the amount of emulsifiers in this food has greatly increased, and at the same time inflammatory diseases such as colitis have also increased.

A new study in the publication Nature looked for connections between these common food additives and diseases in mice, and discovered a link between two of the common ingredients and intestinal disorders.

By disrupting the microbiome found in the gut the emulsifiers increased the chances of digestive problems, highlighting the importance of our internal ecosystem to our overall health. The two ingredients in question had what I considered quite poetic names, and I felt compelled to make this observation in my comment.

Consider Your Lining When Dining

Taking care of your microbiome
May help suppress metabolic syndrome,
So be on your guard and heed the signs
Of pro-inflammatory cytokines.
Ensure you do not overdose
On carboxymethylcellulose,
(And please make sure you're not too matey
With that polysorbate-80),

You'll stay thinner and have more fun
With a healthy epithelium.

SAM MACHKOVECH, AUG 15, 2015

Drones used to monitor bears send their heart rates through the roof

Studying the natural behaviour of animals can be tricky, particularly if the animals in question react to the presence of the humans watching them. With the advent of modern technology some researchers have tried using cameras mounted on drones to observe their subjects, with promising early results, as there seemed to be little or no reaction to the unmanned overhead observers.

In order to test whether this observational technique actually was as un-intrusive as hoped, researchers fitted several wild bears with heart rate monitors and then repeatedly flew a drone over them. The cardiac traces revealed that, while the bears showed little visible reaction to the drones, their heart rates suffered spikes during every over-flight, indicating a heightened level of stress.

Based on these findings, the authors of the paper published in Current Biology recommended carefully considering the possibly invisible effects that drone surveillance might have on wildlife that is being studied.

For myself there was only one possible comment to make on such a story, and it sounds just a little like a brilliant song from a Disney film.

Not Their Necessities

Look for the – drone – that's buzzin' you,
That's being flown by someone who
Is monitoring your cardiac distress!

I mean the – drone – that's watching you
When you're alone and on the loo,
Creating an insomniac with stress!

Where-ever you wander,
Where-ever you roam,
You'll never escape them,
They'll follow you home!

The drones are buzzin' in the trees
To take some photographs of me,
While I look under the rocks and plants
It sneaks up behind and makes me shit my pants,

So what're you going to do?
The drones of Skynet, they'll be coming soon for you,
(coming for you), they'll come for YOU!

JENNIFER OUELLETTE, MAY 13. 2021

New analysis confirms hypothesis for source of mysterious auroral "dunes"

The Earth is constantly being bombarded with charged particles from the Sun, and at the poles these are channelled by our magnetic field into more intense streams.

When these streams collide with oxygen and nitrogen molecules in the atmosphere it can cause the molecules to glow, creating the phenomena we know as the northern or southern lights.

In one rare form these lights take on a rolling, wave-like structure known as an auroral dune, and researchers have now published evidence seemingly confirming the theory proposed to account for these rare observations.

The theory involves the formation of a waveguide between layers of the atmosphere, that in turn creates an atmospheric phenomena known as a mesospheric bore, that then creates waves of high and low pressure oxygen atoms, that finally creates the dune-like light display.

Impressively killing two birds with a single stone, my comment managed to mangle not just this interesting article, but also a well known passage by a well known bard.

Galileo and Juliet

Soft! What light from yonder window breaks?
No soft'ning glow nor rawer aura, but
An aurora bore aloft, by the borealis bore! Ah,
Mesospheric wave, guide me to shore,
Where dunes of light delight me more!

(c) Bill Shakesgeezer

ROSE EVELETH, NOV 27, 2021

It's time to fear the fungi

Fungal spores are extremely small, small enough that they can stay suspended in the air, and fungi produce vast quantities of them. This helps explain why they can be found almost everywhere, and infect creatures from fish to bats to humans.

The reason humans aren't subject to more frequent fungal infections is thanks to our hot-blooded nature; fungi prefer cooler conditions and most of them cannot survive our internal body heat.

This fortunate situation may however not last much longer, thanks to climate change, according to a theory proposed by a researcher at Johns Hopkins University. As more of the world warms and approaches normal human body temperature, more viruses will evolve to withstand the new conditions, and ones that previously found us too hot might then find us just right, with fatal consequences.

The prospect of a well-known insect killing fungus appearing in humans was enough to prompt my rather gloomy comment.

Who Foretold The Mould?

If fungi ruin your fun, guy,
and mushrooms grow out of your head,
Then you might wonder why, guy
(at least until you are dead).
Lend me your ears while they work, guy,
and I will explain the cause:
It's a fungus making you jerk, guy,
just so it can spread all its spores.
You think you're so clever and bold, guy,
but really I'm afraid that you aren't.
You just succumbed to some mould, guy,
killed by a "simplistic" plant.
Enjoy your peace while it lasts, guy,
and take the appropriate steps,
To avoid my gloomy forecasts, guy,
of a human-infecting cordyceps.

JENNIFER OUELLETTE, JAN 17, 2022

Over 100 different species made this 2,200-year-old shipwreck home, study finds

After recovering several relics of an ancient sea battle from the seabed of the Mediterranean, scientists analysed one item – a bronze ram – and discovered that there were over one hundred species of sea life making the long-forgotten object their home.

The scientists noted that the ram served as a kind of "ecological memory" of colonisation, which is surely an important area of study. The point that didn't seem to be mentioned in the article was the other side of this coin – the uncounted members of the over one hundred species that died when their home was dragged unceremoniously from where it had peacefully lain for over two millennia just so some scientists could have a look at it.

I decided to rectify this unfortunate omission with my comment.

No Finer Diner

Encrusted in crustaceans I admire the cetaceans
that pass me by,
Until "Good grief, I'm now a reef!"
as on my submerged bed I lie.
I've stayed too long and now belong
to the class "commissariat",
To humans I'm an artefact, to others just as worthy
I am simply habitat.

BETH MOLE, JAN 18, 2022

COVID-infected hamsters in pet shop trigger animal cull in Hong Kong

After a worker in a Hong Kong pet shop became infected with the Delta strain of Covid-19, when the prevailing variant in the area was the Omicron strain, authorities discovered that the recently imported hamsters in the shop were infected with Covid.

Unable to rule out interspecies transmission they ordered a cull of about 2,000 small mammals, and issued public health guidance to owners of similar animals.

I could have commented on the arrogance of a species that treats other living things as property to be used or murdered at need, but I must have been in an unusually positive mood as what I actually posted was a little lighter in tone.

Worstiality

Loving your pet is just dandy,
and feeding is surely alright, but
Whatever you do (lest Covid ensue) –
don't kiss your hamster goodnight.

JENNIFER OUELLETTE, OCT 5, 2023

We now know how cats purr—why they purr is still up for debate

Most smaller cats can purr, most larger cats can roar – no cat can do both. While the roaring mechanism is thought to be due to the specific bone structure of  roaring cats, the ways in which small creatures like domestic moggies could produce low-frequency noises like purrs was not clearly understood.

By passing air through the excised larynxes of eight, fortunately euthanized cats, researchers were able to produce purring sounds from all of them, showing that the sound isn't created by muscle activity outside the throat, as those muscles were missing in their test.

The article went into great detail on this interesting subject, but raised an equally interesting question – *why* do cats purr? A question that I thought had actually been at least partially answered by one of the first "funny cat pics"[2], as I sought to point out with my comment.

---
[2] His Lordship, the Right Honourable, the Earl Catfood of Ashford.

I Purr Because ...

The sun is warm, my belly's full, a hand upon my fur,
A little milk, or even cream – 'cos that's what I prefer.
I think you'll find like all my kind I is a connoisseur,
Or a piece of string could be the thing
that convinces me to purr.

A squeaky mouse, a friendly house, admiring my coiffeur,
A piece of cheese, not having fleas, being a big poseur,
Having a fight, always being right, 'cos to be human's to err,
And you can be sure that I'll give a purr
if I *can* has cheezburger.

VIVIANE CALLIER, OCT 29, 2023

Where the heck did all those structures inside complex cells come from?

Complex, multicellular life differs from its unicellular cousins not just in the number of cells making a lifeform but in their complexity. And as the eukaryotic cells of complex life have features found in both simple archaeal cells and simple bacterial cells the current theory for how eukaryotic cells arose involves one simple cell engulfing another.

Specifically it is thought that an ancient archaeal cell engulfed an alphaproteobacteria cell, creating the mitochondria found today inside eukaryotic cells. This might generally explain how complex cells came about, but there are competing theories regarding the specifics of how this event led to the creation of all of the complex structures found within these cells today.

This article, republished from Knowable Magazine, goes into great detail on these theories, and manages to explain the intricate biochemistry at work in an easily digestible form. It does however span four or five pages, and I thought I could sum it up a little more succinctly, hence my comment.

Look Inside

The protobacteria are to blame –
their alpha committed the sin.
Wanna know why we're all the same?
The answer eukarywithin.

ELIZABETH RAYNE, DEC 18, 2023

Tracking the genes that turn a fungus into a carnivore

The normal prey of the fungus *Arthrobotrys oligospora* are pieces of dead wood, but if a wandering nematode worm wanders too close then the fungus transforms into a worm-munching monster.

This article explains how a team of researchers in Taiwan studied the genetic changes that allow this simple organism to transition from a saprotrophic to a carnivorous diet.

They found that when the fungus detects a worm its hyphae initially excrete proteins that act as worm glue, and then produce enzymes that allow the fungus to consume its helpless victim alive.

Many interesting stories could be told about this fascinating and ancient relationship; instead I turned to an old Elvis classic for my comment.

Delicious Binds

I'm caught in a trap. I can't go back.
Because your hyphae are so sticky.
You'll eat me alive. Just so you can thrive.
I bet humans find that quite icky.

But we'll go on together.
For millions of years.
We may not last forever –
But we'll outlive our peers.

JENNIFER OUELLETTE, DEC 27, 2023

Getting to the bottom of how red flour beetles absorb water through their butts

Reporting on an article in PNAS, this story describes how researchers have studied the biological mechanisms that allow the red flour beetle to survive in extremely arid conditions, without ever actually drinking any water.

It achieves this impressive feat with specialised cells that can transport potassium chloride, and kidneys that can accumulate very high concentrations of salts, enabling them to absorb all of the moisture in the beetle's dung. And when the humidity is high the beetle can open its rectum and absorb moisture from the atmosphere.

You might initially think that this amazing ability might one day potentially be of use to humans, so that we could survive in an arid environment such as Mars (possibly *without* the bottom-breathing), however this research was aimed at working out how best to kill the pesky beetles, because they like to eat the same food that we do.

I could have emphasised this unmentioned angle to the story in my comment, instead I found the beetle's biology itself to be rather poetic, though I'm not sure anyone else would agree.

Defecation Desiccation

Malpighian tubules do their work in the perirectal space,
As the perinephric membrane helps remove every last trace
Of water from the beetle's dung, and air in its back road;
If it sat in a puddle would the poor thing then explode?

"Go suck water through your butt"
sounds like that yellow Bart,
But evolution knows a trick, it's pretty bloody smart.
If where you live is just too dry then use water in the air,
Absorbed by all the halide salts found in your derrière.

BETH MOLE, FEB 12, 2024

Rare bubonic plague case in Oregon spread from very sick pet cat

Relating how a pet owner in the western US was infected with the plague virus by their cat, this article could make worrying reading for any other indentured servants of our feline overlords.

Reassuringly cases of this famously unpleasant disease are not only rare but treatable, and the human victim responded well to antibiotics; unfortunately the story fails to tell readers the fate of the poorly puss.

Public health officials in the area provided some prosaic advice; I thought I could provide it in more poetic form. I'm not sure I succeeded.

Even Worstiality

If your moggy feels groggy you really should fret,
And whisk Mr. Whiskers straight off to the vet.
It may seem as if he's just out of breath,
But check that he hasn't passed on the Black Death.

DIANA GITIG, MAY 10, 2024

Variant of a toad-based psychedelic can act as an antidepressant

While my comment to this article is actually almost on-topic for a change, dealing as it does with toads, the article goes into some detail on how the potential therapeutic effects of genetically-modified variants of the psychedelic drug produced by the Colorado River toad were tested.

This involved bullying mice, or at least letting some mice get bullied, and then drugging them with untested compounds to see what effects these had on the stressed-out rodents. I'm sure I could have found something to say about this experiment from the point of view of the poor mice; instead in a break from my usual off-topic ramblings I felt compelled to note that there are several ways to read the words "toad hallucinogen".

In hindsight this isn't actually very useful or amusing, but it was the best I could come up with at the time.

Mr Toad Takes A Trip

"Well bless my clogs, I'm seeing frogs,
I'm seeing frogs again!"
Well, not quite that kind of toad hallucinogen,
Or even one that makes amphibians hallucinate,
(Causing them to involuntarily aestivate).

If you feel down then maybe these folk know the cause:
It's all because of your serotonin receptors,
Just grab a toad (a GM toad), then lick your fingertips
And see if you still feel depressed
when you get back from your trips.

NALA ROGERS, MAY 10, 2024

The wasps that tamed viruses

First appearing in Knowable Magazine, this article brings readers possibly unwanted details on how some wasps enlist the help of viruses in order to subdue their caterpillar prey. This in turn allows their eggs to hatch into maggots that consume the helpless caterpillars from the inside out.

The wasp contains within its own DNA copies of so-called domesticated viruses, which it produces in large quantities in its ovaries. These viral particles are then injected into its victims along with the eggs, where they act to suppress the host's immune system, rendering it unable to avoid becoming living baby food.

As might be expected, many of the comments before mine noted how unpleasant this seemed from a human perspective – as I personally seem to have difficulty finding that particular perspective my comment was a little less anthropocentric.

Viral Infection By Larval Injection

Eaten alive from inside out whilst helpless to resist,
The very thought makes monkey brains need a psychiatrist,
But it's just another way that things have found to (co)exist,
And as a gardener those caterpillars *won't* be missed.

And yet of all the strategies that creatures have employed,
To help prevent their species being completely destroyed,
The idea of hosting larvae in your intestinal voids,
Makes me somewhat unkeen on endoparasitoids.

JACEK KRYWKO, MAY 22, 2024

Whale songs have features of language, but whales may not be speaking

By analysing a database of the calls of Caribbean sperm whales, a team of researchers at MIT have discovered levels of contextual and combinatorial structures in these inter-whale communications.

The short bursts of clicks, called codas, that the whales use to communicate were previously thought to only consist of 21 different variations, used over and over again. This new analysis showed that the whales are able to vary several aspects of these codas creating over 500 variations, of which about 150 were regularly used.

Disappointingly the story noted that we're still not close to actually being able to communicate with our large aquatic cousins; my disagreement with this assessment was expressed in my comment.

A Song of Ice and Mire

The vocabulary is small, yet it's delivered fortissimo,
Whales have words for water like Eskimos have for snow.

Art is never discussed, and likewise politics
Is never the subject of these cetacean clicks.

When all you ever really see all day is sea,
You don't really need much combinatoriality.

But if you'd like a translation, then I'll grant your wish:
What they're really saying is "Who took our bloody fish?"

SCIENCE

MATTHEW FRANCIS, JUL 13, 2012

Meteorites, not comets, may have brought water to Earth

When the primordial cloud of gas, dust and ice collapsed to form our Solar System, the heavier elements were drawn inwards towards the forming protostar more quickly than the light ones.

One consequence of this was that water molecules have different ratios of deuterium isotopes, that's hydrogen atoms with a neutron, depending on how close to the Sun they formed.

By comparing the ratios of these deuterium isotopes found on Earth, in meteorites and in comets, researchers have concluded that primitive meteorites known as CI chondrites were the most likely water delivery candidates, as they bear the closest resemblance to the primordial components of the terrestrial planets.

This interesting and detailed study prompted me to produce the following somewhat less interesting or detailed response:

Nicer Ice

Jack and Jill went into space to get some H_2O;
Jack a CI chondrite grabbed, but Jill simply said "No",
"I want this stuff to drink" she said,
"and not to run my Chevy",
"We'll get our ice from further out,
where the water ain't so heavy".

MATT FORD, JUL 14, 2012

The fruits of string theory: The Shape of Inner Space

Not so much a science article as a review of a book on String Theory, written by one of the mathematicians responsible for the mathematical proof that underlies the theory.
Unfortunately I wasn't inspired to buy the book – but I was at least inspired to make a comment.

Probably not a particularly useful or insightful comment to be sure, so pretty much par for the course.

The String's The Thing

To physicists string theorists
are simply rabble rousers,
To engineers the string is queer –
(as it won't hold up their trousers),
A geometer can cope better,
but a Buddhist knows what's what:
Just look inside and you will see,
the Universe is Knot!

MATTHEW FRANCIS, JUL 16, 2012

Can non-Newtonian fluid behaviour explain stuck ketchup bottles?

An article on non-Newtonian fluids prompted the question "Is shear-thickening why ketchup won't come out of the bottle if you tap it?". The answer, as revealed by this follow-up story, is actually "no", as ketchup is a *shear-thinning* fluid – unless one were to, e.g. add cornflour to it.

Messing With Dressing

A thixotropic condiment will always be great fun,
Add cornflour to ketchup – and across it you can run.
But don't add it in the bottle and then give the stuff a clout,
For your shear-thickened solution
will be reluctant to come out.
(If your bottle is old-fashioned
and you can't give it a squeeze,
Just tap the 57 to get your sauce out
with great ease, on your peas).

JOHN TIMMER, JUL 21, 2012

Heavy ion collisions reveal the earliest instants of our Universe

The Relativistic Heavy Ion Collider in the US is sometimes joined by the Large Hadron Collider at CERN in smashing together heavy ions, and analysing the results in order to study the fundamental forces of the universe.

Unlike hadron collisions which occur mainly in empty space, the heavy ions are smashed in groups, which means the resulting quarks and gluons form a plasma, and have a chance to interact with each other.

This Quark-Gluon Plasma is thought to resemble the state the universe was in for less than a second after the Big Bang, before it cooled enough to let protons and neutrons form.

I can't actually remember what state I was in when I commented on this fascinating story, but I can tell you it was about the same time as the discovery of the Higgs boson. And I felt strangely bardic.

The Theoretical Physicist of Venice

O hell! What have we here?
A Cyclotron, within whose empty eye
There is a written scroll! I'll read the writing:

"In our splitters is not gold,
(Lead ions are what we were sold)".
"Heat 'em up so they're not cold;
The nascent universe behold!"

"As Mr. Higgs has oft foretold,
Had we been as wise as bold,
His boson we would soon unfold –
Before the poor bloke is too old".

MATTHEW FRANCIS, JUL 24, 2012

Researchers control reactions between just two atoms

Unlike electrically neutral atoms, ions can undergo chemical reactions even at low temperatures. The authors of a new study published in Nature Physics exploited this property by magnetically trapping ytterbium ions and neutral rubidium atoms at very low temperatures, and exciting the ytterbium ions with laser light.

In the experiment, the reactions were all exothermic, meaning the additional internal energy from the excited state could be converted to kinetic energy, so that the products of the reaction moved faster after than they did before. Alternatively, the extra energy could be converted to photons – an example of fluorescence.

One interesting thing the researchers noted: they found that the relative orientation of the electronic spin and the nuclear spin – known as the hyperfine state – made a difference to the reaction outcome.

For reasons that only a psychologist could explain, my mental processes turned this story into a version of an old Billy Joel song. Or tried to, anyway.

Hyperfine State of Mind

Some ions like to interact,
This is a fact that I think you know.
At least we'd expect them to, if they're not too slow.
But if you freeze some ytterbium,
That's not what you'll find,
If it's in a hyperfine state of mind.

Simply mix with rubidium,
In your living room, or your physics lab.
Then you may see it pinch a shell (like a hermit crab).
Just make sure that your ions
Are carefully confined,
If they're in a hyperfine state of mind.

You may think it fantastic,
If inelastic collisions occur.
Reactions are exothermic, I'm sure you'll concur.
Now wait with the lights off
For fluorescence unrefined,
If it's in a hyperfine state of mind.

MATTHEW FRANCIS, MAR 8, 2013

Disentangling photons and atoms to keep quantum systems clean

Reporting on an article in the publication Science, Mr Francis carefully and clearly explains how researchers used measurements of the scattering of laser light from a single trapped strontium atom to measure the effects of decoherence on quantum systems. They discovered that, by varying the angle of the light relative to the spin of the atom some angles were more or less prone to entanglement.

Apparently the only thing I really took from the article was a reminder of a comic book character from my youth.

Here's Johnny!

When your electron's in a spin
And you let a photon in,
The quantum state will soon gyrate –
Decoherence, for the win.

Your magnetic field is bent so
You know where your boson went,
Polarisation's an indication
You have made entanglement.

But if you clear the quantum smog,
And collapse the quantum fog,
The chap you'll see's called Johnny,
(A.k.a. Strontium Dog).

MATTHEW FRANCIS, OCT 23. 2013

New type of quantum excitation behaves like a solitary particle

Reporting on a paper published in Nature, this article clearly explains, in terms that even I could understand, how researchers have, for the first time, created solitary virtual quantum particles called levitons, by passing carefully controlled electrical currents through semiconductors.

While it may not initially sound like it, this subject is so poetic I merely had to re-arrange some of the words to produce my rather abbreviated comment.

A Simple Sentence

Don't let random fluctuations in electromagnetic interactions Mask your quantum excitations (with voltages in fractions) – You'll see leviton realisations with quasi-particular attractions.

Science is just so poetic.

MATTHEW FRANCIS, MAR 9, 2014

Is the lopsided Universe telling us we need new theories?

According to our picture of the Cosmic Microwave Background (a "heatmap" of the entire sky) our universe is just a little bit lopsided, with unexplained asymmetries on scales much larger than any physical structures.

This article looks at several possible explanations proposed by various researchers, covering theories from the mundane to the exotic, possibly requiring changes to our understanding of fundamental physics.

As I've long been fascinated by such things I was inspired to produce a few lines on an almost related subject.

Asymmetricality We Love Thee

For an instant it was perfect – completely error-free,
But perfection is unstable – it simply has to be.
The slightest quantum hiccup will shatter symmetry,
(And thankfully, in the process, create our reality).

But our isotropic cosmos has some features that are bent,
And we've inconclusive data
from the probes we've so far sent,
So now we're finding theories to try and make a dent,
In the unexplained variations in the monopole moment.

The perfect thermal body, for which I feel such love,
The universe! Reality! The great heavens above!
(Only heaven can't be up there 'cos perfection got a shove.
Immortality must be as sterile as a surgeon's glove).

And now temperature fluctuations in spherical harmonics,
Are decomposed by scientists (armed with gin and tonics).
Personally I'd like to give these clever chaps my thanks,
I'd really love to help them –
but I'm as thick as two Max Plancks.

MATTHEW FRANCIS, FEB 21, 2014

Is entanglement real or is there a super-deterministic cosmic conspiracy?

In order to get around some of the "spooky action at a distance" issues that the theory of quantum entanglement produces, some researchers have proposed "hidden variables" that give the *appearance* of entanglement.

To test this theory a paper published in Physical Review Letters proposes using light from two widely separated and distant quasars to initialise quantum experiments, as the photons from each quasar could not have interacted for the life of the universe.

If hidden variables are found to exist it would have consequences for the idea of free will, as it would show that the results of some experiments were actually determined at the start of time – or even before!

Quasars Set To Stun

Well, collapse my waveform, this stuff is brill!
Does anything really have free will,
Or are we pieces of a cosmic clock?
Can anyone else here hear "tick tock"?

Entanglement is just an illusion,
Due to the principle of exclusion,
Our limited understanding of "space":
Two things *cannot* be in one place.

But if one thing can be found in two,
Then what's a physicist to do?
It's enough to make you mad a smidgen,
(Or even turn you to religion!)

The answer as you've read at Ars
Is to be found among quasars,
Unless we pull a hidden variable
From the celestial cotton wool.

SHALINI SAXENA, MAR 26, 2015

Graphene allows strange form of ice to occur at room temperature

Water is great, and also rather weird from a scientific perspective, as its molecules exhibit some unique properties. This article describes how researchers trapped a tiny amount of water between two carbon nanotube lattices, and this caused a novel type of ice to form at room temperature.

Interestingly the carbon lattices caused the angle at which hydrogen bonds formed to change, altering the familiar geometry of ice crystals. Less interestingly, I was inspired to comment with a simple rhyming couplet.

Even Nicer Ice

The latest publicity for carbon nanotubes:
Their hydrophobicity makes perfect ice cubes.

JOHN TIMMER, MAY 14, 2015

Tiny diamonds wrapped in graphene get rid of friction

By sprinkling very tiny diamonds between two surfaces, one of which was coated in graphene, researchers at the Argonne National Lab achieved an almost frictionless state called "superlubricity".

Notably this was the first experiment to demonstrate this effect at larger than microscopic scales, making it of potentially great interest in any facet of life that would benefit from lower friction.

Obvious and useful examples would be mechanical devices such as engines, however for reasons that are probably best left unexplored my comment veered into less obvious territory.

Grapholene!

Are embarrassing friction and intimate stick-tion
problems that you'd like to end?
Then here's the solution! A little ablution
with graphene I would recommend!
The superlubricity is utter simplicity;
your coefficient it will amend,
So as you can see, I'm sure you'll agree,
nanodiamonds are a girl's best friend!

JENNIFER OUELLETTE, OCT 5, 2020

Archaeologists find evidence of neurons in glassy brain of Vesuvius victim

When Mt. Vesuvius erupted, wiping out Pompeii and Herculaneum, most of the inhabitants of those towns were asphyxiated by the toxic clouds of dust and gas, however some succumbed to a pyroclastic blast estimated to have been about 500° Celsius.

This caused the unfortunate victim's skulls to literally explode, with their brains usually suffering "saponification" – or being turned to soap. For a "lucky" few however the heat actually caused "vitrification" – they were turned to glass.

This story caused another song from my youth to pop into my head, which in turn prompted me to post the following comment.

Frozen In Thought

Once I was alive, but then this hot gas,
Soon came along, turned my brain to glass.
Seemed like the real thing, and now you'll find,
There's not much of me, left behind.

Vitrified, the pyroclastic flow has turned me
Glassy inside, now I know I'll always be, crusty outside,
And I fear I'll stay this way,
It's just no good, my final thought was
"Now I'm see-through".

And who knew that Debbie Harry was a palaeoproteomicist?

JOHN TIMMER, JUN 17, 2021

Researchers cool a 40 kg object to near its quantum ground state

In order to detect gravity waves the LIGO detector tries to measure tiny deflections in laser light. To make the detection easier the light is bounced between two mirrors at opposite ends of a long tunnel, greatly increasing the distance it covers.

Because any instability in the mirrors will interfere with the gravity wave detection a damping system is used, which effectively takes energy – and thus heat, out of the mirrors.

In a paper published in Science the researchers estimated that the 40kg mirror contained only eleven phonons – a quantum unit of vibration. This is equivalent to 77 nano-Kelvin, or very close to absolute zero, remarkable for such a large object. And while impressive in itself, the study of quantum effects on large objects could lead to finally fitting gravity into quantum mechanics.

In response to this amazing article I came up with part of a nursery rhyme, and noted that 11 is not 17. So only *slightly* less impressive.

Reflection Perfection

Mirror, mirror, underground,
You're the coolest thing around.
Down in LIGO's basement where
They cool you down to warm the air!

Brrr

Eleven phonons
Colder than winter's bite – a
haiku does not make

JENNIFER OUELLETTE, JUL 8, 2021

What fractals, Fibonacci, and the golden ratio have to do with cauliflower

Reporting on a story in the journal Science, this article describes how researchers used both experimental techniques and computer modelling to study how many plants, particularly noticeably the Romanesco cauliflower, produce their leaves in patterns that follow the Fibonnaci sequence, thus producing fractals – shapes that repeat at many different scales.

While my personal interest in cauliflowers is limited to the edible variety, I did find the mathematical aspects of the story interesting, particularly as I'd recently come across references to the Golden Ratio in what might seem to be a completely unrelated area – unifying relativity and quantum mechanics by creating a theory of quantum gravity.

Cauliflowers and quantum gravity – great universe, huh?

Harmonic Mnemonic

Phee Phi Pho Phum, I know the number that follows One,
I add those two and it makes Three,
Phum and Pho and Phi and Phee!
Repeat this with great frequency to get all Fibo-sequencey,
Divide by previous and you'll know about the Golden Ratio.

JOHN TIMMER, JUL 25, 2021

Marsquakes illuminate what lies beneath the sands of Mars

By studying how seismic waves travel through a planet scientists are able to build up a picture of the composition of the interior, and since NASA landed an earthquake — or marsquake — detector on the red planet data has been gathered on our celestial sister's internal make-up.

From these preliminary results it appears that our neighbour has a large and light core, wonderfully illustrated in the cut-away picture accompanying the story[3]. The ratio of the size of the core to that of the planet, along with the dusky hue, prompted many comments regarding its likeness to a terrestrial treat, and I was also compelled to remark on this similarity. Only *in rhyme.*

---

[3] That image was copyrighted, so I've used a "free" NASA one instead. Sorry. Visit ArsTechnica.com to see the original.

Celestial Fruit

Of Marsquakes we were unawares;
now that data's in reach:
Earth and Moon are apples and pears,
but Mars is just a peach.

JOHN TIMMER, FEB 9, 2022

European project sets a record for fusion energy produced by a tokamak

Nuclear fusion – the process of squashing simple atomic nuclei together to make more complicated ones – holds the promise of nearly limitless clean power. This article reports how, in a facility in Oxford, UK scientists have just set a new record for the amount of power produced using fusion.

Unfortunately this is still less than the power it takes to *create* the fusion, a situation that has endured since the first successful fusion experiments – despite much research and investment. While the article does an excellent job of explaining the process and the hardware, it does so without a single detectable rhyme, a lamentable oversight that I thought I could rectify.

Full Nuclear Ahead to the Steam Age

Now there's some confusion 'bout nuclear fusion
that I'd like to try and address;
An incipient boon that's coming *real* soon –
about 20 years I would guess.

So let me relate why this is so great –
here are some of the facts:
Just take a flat pack Ikea tokamak
and turn all of your magnets to max.

Now make a miasma (just inject some plasma),
then monitor your spectroscopes,
As the magic of heat performs a neat feat
and transforms all of your isotopes.

"And what good is this?" I hear you insist,
"for the free power of which we all dream?"
Well this phenomenon leaves a spare neutron,
and with this we can make – steam!

Yep, boiling water is now how we oughta
make power – no hyperbole.
Now will anyone join me for what may well be
the world's dearest cup of tea?

DHANANJAY KHADLIKAR, AUG 10, 2022

The coolest instrument in space: Building the Webb's MIRI

Following the successful launch and deployment of the James Webb Space Telescope, this article chronicles the genesis of its mid-infrared detector instrument, MIRI.

With quotes from several of the scientists involved in its creation, and fascinating details on its construction, readers are given a glimpse into the technical achievements the instrument represents.

This prompted another reader (Oldmanalex) to post: *"A truly awesome piece of kit, allowing an amazingly sharp view into a hitherto unexplored world. Maybe for astronomers this will be a Cortez in Darien moment. Pity we do not have a Keats to eulogize it."*

I felt compelled to respond that, while Ars didn't have a Keats, it did have a geezer ...

On First Looking Into The Mid-Infrared

Much have I travell'd in the realms of space,
And many goodly stars and planets seen;
With many data readouts on my screen,
Which nerds in fealty to Linus hold.
Oft of one wide expanse had I been told
That deep-brow'd Hawking ruled as his demesne;
Yet did I never breathe its pure serene
Till I saw MIRI's print out loud and bold:
Then felt I like some watcher of the skies
Viewing anew the space where answers dwell,
Or like stout Herschel when, with eagle eyes,
Added Uranus to the celestial carousel.
I'm filled afresh with wonder and surprise,
Thanks to those clever folk at JPL.

ELIZABETH RAYNE, OCT 5, 2023

The snow forecast for Mars: Dry ice and a meter a year

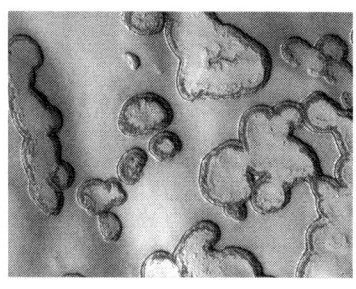

This article relates how a team at Berlin Technical University studied the amount of carbon dioxide snowfall on Mars by analysing the shadows cast by blocks of ice on the surface, as shown in high resolution pictures from the NASA HiRISE experiment.

While some of the processes involved in Martian weather that affect the seasonal snowfall are literally alien, others can be found in terrestrial situations, such as the swirling "katabatic" winds caused by descending cold air.

The article subject is certainly interesting in and of itself, however the accompanying picture[4] showing the Martian South Pole covered in snow, with the terrain outlined in golden tones, is absolutely striking. Early comments on the article noted that these features resembled varves, layered structures created by rivers on Earth depositing silt.

---

[4] Image thanks to NASA/JPL

I was inspired to wax poetic – or at least as close to poetic as I could manage.

And Now The Weather

... so the sullen sky paints dusky red across the barren view of deserts (and an old lake bed), and snow of CO_2.
Bi-chromatic white-brown halves,
as though palomino skinned;
the organic topology of varves, stirred by katabatic wind.

JOHN TIMMER, NOV 1, 2023

Remains of planet that formed the Moon may be hiding near Earth's core

The current theory for how our moon came to be involves a Mars-sized planet called Theia crashing into the early Earth, consequently sending enough material into orbit to create our lunar partner.

Reporting on a paper published in Nature, this article describes how pieces of this lost planet might have ended up deep inside the Earth, causing the two, otherwise unexplained "low velocity" zones within the mantle – areas where seismic waves are slowed down.

Due to the obviously erratic functioning of my brain I felt compelled to try and fit these interesting findings into a 1960s Bacharach classic.

Lunar Tessera Interred in Terra

Whenever I look down,
And try to see beneath the ground,
I find a piece of Theia in you.

Though it's rocky and dusty,
And outside it's rather crusty,
I see a piece of Theia in you.

Forever, forever, you'll stay in my core, and I will keep you,
Forever, forever, deep beneath my floor, I will contain you,
Together, together, that's how it must be, to live without you
Would only mean planetary breakup for me.

.

ERIC BERGER, MAY 21, 2024

Daily Telescope: Black holes have been merging for a long, long time

This article is focused solely on an image produced by the Near-Infrared Spectrograph instrument on the James Webb Space Telescope. The image shows two galaxies, and the massive black holes at their centres, merging just 740 million years after the Big Bang.

For some reason I found this story rather romantic, and commented accordingly.

To Be Hole

When one hole meets another, *of course* they will attract,
James Webb has confirmed that this is an age-old fact.
Nothing wants to be alone, and tell me: what could be
More lonely than to be a singularity?

But this then begs the question:
what to call them when they're merged?
When inertia is absorbed and gravity wells converged?
Quantum maths is weird, for one plus one is one,
But love stories like this
are what make our universe such fun.

KYLE ORLAND, JUL 18, 2012

NASA partners with Microsoft to launch its first launch video game

The Mars Curiosity Rover is an astonishing machine, and the way in which it arrived at the red planet was equally astonishing, involving as it did being lowered to the surface from a rocket-powered sky-crane.

To both commemorate this remarkable achievement, and also inspire interest in science and space, NASA partnered with game developers from Microsoft to release a free video game to Xbox360 owners, that allows players to try to land a virtual rover themselves.

Now at the same time that this story appeared the media was also reporting on international industrial espionage, with accusations that the recent Chinese advances in space technology were due to "unauthorised borrowing" from the western inventors.

And finally I should point out to those unfamiliar with Ars Technica, the publication claims to be brought to the readership from an orbiting headquarters – an enviable posting if true.

Lander Plunder

Crash! Game Over!
Now my rover's
going to clover
on the sands of Mars.

I'm out of luck
and truly stuck;
no breakdown truck
out here among the stars.

Made in the States
by NASA's greats
(and a few mates),
the tech's worthy of applause.

But though it's tiny,
because it's shiny,
the cunning Chinee
will get their hands on ours.

Orbital HQ –
Enjoy your view;
you lucky few,
the space people of Ars!

JAMES HOLLOWAY, MAR 15, 2013

Meet Yeti, the South Pole's crevasse-detecting robot

Finding cracks in ice sheets is easy. Finding cracks in ice sheets *without* falling in them is a bit harder. As such the job of mapping potentially dangerous cracks can be time-consuming and tedious, making it an ideal candidate for robotic replacement.

And lo! Meet Yeti, an 80 kg wheeled robot armed with both GPS, so it knows where it is, and GPR – Ground Penetrating Radar so it can detect crevasses. Running on lithium-ion batteries kept warm by chemical hand-warmers, the robot is built from stock parts, a fact lamented by its operator, who noted that wider custom-made wheels would improve its ability to traverse the snow.

The robot can be controlled manually if it runs into an occasional obstacle (as it cannot "see" by itself), otherwise it follows a preprogrammed rosette-shaped course around its target search area. The curved paths allow the robot to approach any crevasses from multiple angles, making them easier to spot on the radar, and its small size means it can cross snow bridges that wouldn't support a larger vehicle.

This was particularly relevant at the time this story appeared, as it coincided with yet another politically-motivated US government shutdown, which then led to the Americans having to resupply their south polar bases by land rather than air.

For better or worse it was this synchronicity that formed the basis of my comment.

Cracking Tracking, Tracking Cracking / (Smallfoot)

The land of the free (where little is) was hit by sequestration,
And now they can't afford to fly stuff
to their South Pole station.
Now some poor Joe has the nice job
of visiting them by truck,
Across the broken ice sheets –
and *without* them getting stuck.

This really isn't easy, as the cracks are hard to see,
Covered on the surface (like those in the economy).
What you need's a robot to search each and every section,
Or, in other words, some autonomous crevasse detection.

When viewed from space the robots trail
looks like petals unfurled,
Drawing flower-shaped crop circles
at the bottom of the world.
This GPS geometry, while blind, is really neat,
But to really do its job this Yeti needs bigger feet.

CHRIS KEALI, JAN 19, 2014

Kim Dotcom's answer to Spotify and iTunes – Baboom – will soft launch on Monday

One of the many notable changes that the Internet has wrought on society is the transition from distributing digital media on small, shiny discs, to it being delivered via online streaming. This transition was not however exactly smooth – or even voluntary, and the period is marked by the rise of P2P file sharing services such as Napster, Kazaa and Mega.

Created by a video gamer and self-proclaimed hacker from Germany, who had changed his name to Kim Dot Com, the Mega file sharing service was a thinly veiled fair-use cover over a platform that enabled mass copyright infringement.

In doing so it just happened to make Mr Dot Com lots and lots of money from advertising, and he moved to New Zealand, bought a mansion and started a parallel "career" as a rapper.

Things didn't exactly go smoothly however, with the US requesting his extradition, and the New Zealand police raiding said mansion, where Mr Dot Com had taken refuge in a panic room.

This article records how Mr Dot Com, despite these seeming setbacks, still planned to launch a successor to Mega – it would be a music streaming service called BaBoom, and the first artist to be featured would be none other than Mr Dot Com. The launch would however have to be a "soft" one, as his planned public mega party launch event had had to be cancelled.

I could have written a comment with a detailed and in-depth look at the pros and cons of intellectual property laws, instead I simply found Mr Dot Com so obnoxious that I wrote a rather obnoxious comment, though I have a feeling he's probably not the Ars reader type.

Dotcom Begone

A fat white hacker rapper – tell me you're kidding, please!
– Someone send him far away – to the Antipodes.

Oh wait, you already did? And they don't want him too?
What's a poor white hacker rapper mega-boy to do?

I suppose he could mega-hack the latest online fads,
And make some mega-money serving unwanted online ads,

(And bring those US industries to their trembling knees,
By "stealing" all their valuable, sought-after IPs).

And now they've stopped him having fun
playing in the parks,
(Possibly because he's swallowed mega-Bubba Sparxxx).

Poor little mega-boy in his panic room,
Waiting for the police to make the door go ba-BaBoom!

CASEY JOHNSTON, NOV 13, 2014

Taylor Swift wages a campaign against ad-supported music streaming

In 2014 Taylor Swift was a megastar, though few back then would have predicted the heights to which this stardom would rise. This fame and fortune gave her not only a public platform, but leverage when dealing with the streaming services that distributed her music.

This article relates how Spotify in particular caused her ire by playing her work on their ad-supported tier. This, she claimed, made it appear as if her music was of little or no value, as the service was free, a view she took particular exception to.

Ms Swift told the Wall Street Journal: "*Music is art, and art is important and rare. Important, rare things are valuable. Valuable things should be paid for.*"

It shouldn't take too much thought to uncover the fallacy in this statement, but in case it passed you by, art is *not* actually rare. Even "valuable" art, e.g. art that people are willing to pay money for is not that uncommon, and it represents but a tiny fraction of all of the music, paintings, sculptures and other art that the human race constantly creates. I thought that my comment could illustrate this point[5].

(And considering I wrote this ten years ago, it's still fairly accurate.)

---

[5] Dear Swifties, Ms. Swift has brought more pleasure to more people than I ever will, which is laudable. I just think that she could bring about as much joy to the world *without* having tours that cause carbon emissions equivalent to a small country, and if she gave away 95% of her fortune she'd see absolutely no difference in her quality of life, but tens of thousands of other lives could be completely transformed, or even saved. I don't like billionaires – sorry Taylor.

The Last Swift of Autumn

2/4 Country Rhythm
|C |Dm |G |F |

I first met you on the Internet (I don't watch much TV),
I saw your name in an article on music piracy.
My first thought was you were a bloke – or real quick at making suits,
But no, you're actually a girl, with country music roots.
And then it clicked you were the one that Kanye interrupted,
(And who is he? I'd no idea until you were disrupted).

CHORUS – REPEAT BETWEEN VERSES
|G |Am |Em Em/G |C |

I'm out of touch, and out of tune, and no-one here loves me,
|F |Dm7 |G G7 |C |

And what is more I must be mad – I wrote this song for free!

And now you're back in the headlines; Taylor, I cannot lie,
If it wasn't for your news I'd never have heard of Spotify.
I've never heard your music and I probably never will,
But as a fellow "artist" I appreciate your ill
Feelings towards them. (Did you see what I did there?
Widow-orphan rhyming – and I don't. Even. Care!).

Your personal fortune is "merely" one fifth a billion,
No wonder you're upset at only getting half a million,

From people who themselves are worth even more than you,
And they never had to write a song,
or sleep with a vampire too.
And then write yet another song about no vampire sex,
As yet another sing-a-long about your latest ex.

And now this is the final verse – I always love this part,
A chance to leave my audience
with appreciation for my "art",
So dooby-doo and rinky-dink and sha-la-la-la-la,
I've something something love a lot and something from afar!
Oh dooby-doo and Scooby Doo and oh you make me cry,
I'll be a country music fan until the day I expand my musical horizons a bit.

REPEAT CHORUS TO FADE

Art! It's Rare! And Valuable!

LEE HUTCHINSON, JUL 22, 2015

Gallery: we tear apart a $340 audiophile Ethernet cable and look inside

Not so much a product review as a product evisceration, this article literally and figuratively tears apart what claims to be an "audiophile" ethernet cable, for the pleasure of its readers – and the general common good.

The AudioQuest Vodka network cable in question is one and a half metres long and costs $340, or at least ten times as much as a non-audiophile cable of similar quality and length.

My ears, much like my palate, are of the unrefined variety, being completely unable to detect the imperceptible claimed improvements that apparently only astonishingly priced equipment is able to provide, and I thought that my comment should reflect this.

The Emperor's New Cables

Is your Fi not quite as Hi due to your wire's conduction?
Do you fear that you cannot hear an honest reproduction?
Then fret no more, just open your wallet for my inspection,
If I can see you'll meet my fee I'll fix your wire's direction.

All that jitters is not gold – so silver is used instead,
Imbued with properties untold, to get sounds to your head.
And our foil wraps stop any scraps
from leaking to the ether, and
By travelling in style the bits all smile
when they get back together.

And when we're done (if you've still funds)
I'll show you my best line:
Imperial wear as light as air, suitable for the divine!
This gown's so light you need "true" sight to even make it out,
It's really great to separate the refined from the louts.

You *can* see it, can you not? For you *are* a man of taste,
I'd hate to think you'd lost the plot,
that would be such a waste!

TIM DE CHANT, JUL 28, 2021

Facebook's metaverse gambit is a distraction from its deep-seated problems

This story relates how Mark Zuckerberg, the CEO and founder of the so-called social media platform Facebook, announced the company's plans to create the Metaverse, an interactive online version of the Internet where people would spend their lives – and their money – interacting as digital avatars in VR.

At the time of this article Facebook was facing increased legal scrutiny, particularly in the US, for a variety of reasons, and this article presents the theory that the timing of the Metaverse announcement was at least partly an attempt to draw attention away from these potentially serious issues.

The article also followed shortly after news that some Meta VR headsets – made by Facebook's parent company, were causing an allergic reaction in some users.

The idea of the human race spending their lives strapped into VR goggles living in a digital hellscape, where your every interaction is monitored and monetised didn't go down well with the Ars commentariat, however I think that I was the only poster who commented in the form of a rather profane punk-rock song.

The Betterverse

Hey there Zuck you slimy fuck, how's life in Uncanny Valley?
I think your Meta would be better
shoved right up your back alley.

You got my cash – I got the rash your toxic product gave me.
Your fingers curled around my world,
won't someone please come save me?

Your algorithms cause deep schisms In the fabric of society;
But you've no concern if the whole world burns,
and it won't be better in 3D.

You show your greed in each news feed,
and every status update,
Misinformation across the nation, spreading fear and hate.

Please keep your shit, you pasty git,
with your personality bypass,
So take a hike – I've clicked "Dislike",
please shove FB up your arse!

Yes take Facebook you slimy crook,
off from this world of mine,
And place it where I think it's fair to say the sun *don't* shine.

JIM SALTER, AUG 24, 2021

President Biden to host infosec roundtable with tech giant CEOs

After a long series of high profile security breaches affecting large parts of the US population, Bloomberg reported that President Joe Biden invited the CEOs of the largest tech companies to a round table meeting at the White House to discuss the issue.

Writing this summary with a few years hindsight it would seem that little came of the meeting, and my contemporaneous comment reflected my low expectations of governmental solutions to tech problems, rather than any personal animosity.

I quite like 46.

Slomo Joe

... and Uncle Joe said to the suits,
"Sons, your software's leaky".
"I'm sorry, did you say something?
My ears are a bit creaky".
But before a single word was heard
the lawyers jumped right in,
(Like an a-cappella group,
but with pallid, sallow skin):
"Mr POTUS please understand
we're blameless for these disasters,
And pass that on to Joe Public –
so say your lords and masters".
"For he who controls the US of A
is he who controls the trough".
But Uncle Joe did not reply –
the president had nodded off.

SAMUEL AXON, SEP 13, 2021

Apple fixes security vulnerabilities in new versions of iOS, macOS, and watchOS

The content of this article is almost entirely adequately summed up in just the heading, the only other detail of note being that the security patches stopped attackers taking over devices using maliciously crafted PDF files.

My comment does however require some further explanation. I dislike all mega-corporations, on the simple basis that power without accountability is a bad thing for most humans, as the humans who hold this power usually have a proven record of acting in their own self interest, and not in the public good.

What's that got to do with a security update for a mobile phone? Obviously not much, but hopefully it makes clear that I'm only singling out this particular mega-corp as they were the subject of this particular article.

I also have to apologise for recycling an old, rude and rather poor joke – I usually like my work to be nobody's fault but mine, but this was the best I could come up with at the time[6].

---

[6] If you find that this rhyme irks you, there is one later on (the Dragon Man skull one) that may restore some balance. Then again, it may not!

iFail

When is my phone not my phone?

Do you think that you can guess?

It's when my phone is an iPhone, and I've viewed a PDF.

(Note: *my* phone is on Android, if you'll beg my pardon,

Personally I don't like being stuck in a walled garden).

Of course no device is immune to software bugs,

But for overpriced crap for arseholes,

get a gold-plated butt plug.

ERIC BERGER, OCT 13, 2021

At the age of 90, Captain f'n Kirk is finally going to space today

As a supposed adult I am *not* actually a Trekkie (I think the best Star Trek film is Galaxy Quest), but I grew up watching and loving the original series, and have a bit of a soft spot for the actors from that iconic programme.

So it was with a little trepidation that I learned that William Shatner, the actor who played Captain Kirk, would be taking a ride into space on the New Shepard launch vehicle built by Blue Origin, the rocket company created by Jeff Bezos, the founder of Amazon.

Fortunately my fears were misplaced, as Mr Shatner, along with his three co-passengers, were safely returned to Earth after a few minutes in space.

In the article Mr Berger notes that, while the flight provides great publicity for Blue Origin, it doesn't actually address any of the issues the company apparently faces, including missed delivery deadlines, failed bids and a sexist, toxic workplace culture.

Commenting before the flight took off, I simply had to express my concern for Mr Shatner's welfare, given the less-than stellar track record of the company providing his ride. Pun intended.

To Boldly Go...

Now you may know I'm a contrarian
(and also a bit of a jerk),
But I do envy the nonagenarian
actor we know as Kirk.
I just hope the tech bro book seller
doesn't blow him to shreds,
I really don't want the chubby old fella
raining down over all of our heads.

JOHN TIMMER, DEC 2, 2021

Getting software to "hallucinate" reasonable protein structures

In this, one of the earlier articles on the applications of A.I., we learn how a large team of researchers has used the technology to investigate potential protein structures through a process of iteration and alteration.

Despite only being artificial and not actually intelligent, the neural network models that power so-called A.I. *can* actually be used for a variety of useful purposes, and comparing vast numbers of combinations of amino acid chains to some prespecified criteria happens to be one of them.

Unfortunately the software was not able to tell what, if anything, the potential new proteins might do, however the researchers did successfully create some of the structures in the lab, suggesting that the so-called hallucinations were at least on the right track. The term hallucination as applied to A.I. comes from earlier research that used the technology to create an *almost* banana-like picture using the same iterate / alter technique, starting only from random noise.

While I found these results a little disappointing, the prospect of a future where humanity had mastered the machinery of life has been the subject of much sci-fi speculation, and this scenario formed the basis of my comment. Due to my entirely frivolous and unserious nature I found it necessary to use a comic book character in my rhyme, so some further explication is required for the more mature.

If you are unfamiliar with the Marvel comic book characters The Guardians of the Galaxy, one of the unlikelier heroes is a motile tree-like being called Groot, brilliantly brought to life in the Marvel movies by what is possibly Vin Diesel's finest acting performance.

Groot's Roots?

Give big boys toys and some random noise
and they'll hallucinate – some fruit?
I'll be impressed when their field test
introduces itself as "Groot".
Yep, a talking tree would impress me,
if created gene by gene,
Will it not be grand when we understand
the rules shaping protein?
You can place your bets on designer pets
and babies made to order,
When we've got to grips with those cunning strips
of chemical disorder.

JENNIFER OUELLETTE, JAN 4, 2022

Jurassic-period ammonite fossils flex their muscles in virtual 3D

While it may seem as if a story about ammonites and armoured worms should belong in the Nature category of this book, this article goes into some detail on the very technical methods used to scan the fossilised remains of these prehistoric creatures.

These technologies included photography, scanning electron microscopy, energy-dispersive X-ray spectroscopy, neutron tomography and X-ray microtomography, and when their results were combined it produced a more detailed picture of the fossil's interior than any previously seen.

It had been thought that the most ammonoid creature currently extant was the Nautilus, however the new study revealed inner muscular details more similar to colloids – that is the family that includes squids and cuttlefish.

My comment could have referred to the amazing technological advances that led to these discoveries, but I've long thought that ammonites were an extremely impressive and successful creature, and my post reflected this feeling.

Ammonite Acolyte

For half a billion years evolution's holy grail,
Had neither arms nor ears; it was basically a snail.
Now it's grown arms and lost its shell,
is it time to make a fuss?
Don't be alarmed if I foretell the Age of the Octopus!
(Assuming we, that's you and me,
at least give them a chance,
To survive the climate tragedy caused by our arrogance).

KYLE ORLAND, APR 1, 2022

Game dev group says addressing NFT gaming's "ethical issues" is a "priority"

The International Game Developers Association is an industry group with thousands of members from around the world, and this article tells us how they're becoming increasingly concerned by the rise of crypto-like elements in modern gaming.

As I have the luxury of writing this summary with a couple of years hindsight I'm glad to report that non-fungible tokens and other blockchain nonsense generally failed spectacularly in the gaming space, with several publishers trying, and then quickly discarding the idea.

Obviously at the time of the article I had only the hope that this would be the eventual outcome, so my comment merely expressed my general disdain for this buzzword-laden tech idiocy, that has to be one of the most stupid ways that humans are destroying their only home.

Profanity alert!

Blockchain Gravy Train

I give you my dollars, I give you my time,
Yet still you come back for my nickels and dimes,
I know you MBAs feel no shame,
But give me a break, I've paid for the game.
I don't care how much you've got in your banks,
NFTs? No Fucking Thanks.

JON BRODKIN, MAY 10, 2022

Elon Musk would let Trump back on Twitter, says ban was "morally wrong"

Written before Mr Musk completed his takeover of Twitter, this article reports how the billionaire would reverse the platform's previous permanent ban of Donald Trump, which was put into place after his supporters launched a failed insurrection following his loss in the 2020 election.

I am not a fan of billionaires or Nazis generally, so despite the fact that he has some ideas that appeal to the teenage sci-fi fan who still lives inside me I'm really not a fan of Mr Musk specifically.

As he seems to figuratively live on another planet to me currently, and literally wants to live on another planet to me in the future, I doubt I'll ever get the chance to express my opinions to him personally, but Ars are kind enough to provide a platform where I can annoy other people with them, and this article seemed like as good a place as any to post them.

For some reason on this particular day I felt the need to express myself in something approximating rap, possibly because that medium lends itself well to using expletives for emphasis or effect.

Muskrat Rap

Now I'm Lone Skum n' I'm really rich,
Hundred dollar bills are my bed sheets!
Everybody's gonna end up my bitch,
Hey little boy, would you like some tweets?
Check out my tunnel, it won't be boring;
Ride my wheels n' I'll take you to space,
My legacy's gonna be so enduring,
I bet you're already fuckin' sick of my face!
As long as you pay I'll be your pal,
(Unless you try and diss my stuff),
Geniuses like me have our own rationale,
And no, I can never. Have. Enough!

SCHARON HARDING, JUL 6, 2022

Meta highlights NFT, blockchain hopes as it shutters its Novi crypto wallet

Meta, the company best known for Facebook and its CEO Mark Zuckerberg, announced that it will close its crypto wallet Novi in September 2022, and users should empty their wallets as soon as possible to avoid any losses, according to this article from July of that year.

This follows from the failed plans to launch their own crypto coin, which was to have been called, apparently unsarcastically, "Diem" – the enjoyment of the pleasures of the moment without concern for the future. In a way it's a shame the planned coin failed, as the name seems to perfectly encapsulate the attitudes of those who sing the praises of crypto, blockchain and other such fool's gold gibberish.

Unfortunately, despite their setbacks in this area, Meta and Mr Zuckerberg were apparently still keen to press ahead with the new technology in other ways. I suppose I can see the appeal of having your own currency when apparently you think you're the reincarnation of a Roman Emperor, and it was this thought that formed the basis of my comment.

Crypto Through the Tulips

"Bring me a coin, and call it 'free',
because, you know, it ain't",
"And on one side we'll picture – me!
Now wouldn't that be quaint".
"And now I must try and explain,
how this money will be locked",
"You see we wrap it in a chain,
and then the chain is blocked!"
"Of course we'll give you a receipt," –
the Emperor has spoken!
"And it will be this really neat
non-fungible token".
Just wait, and I think you will see
how the Zuck makes it all better,
When we're all products in "web3"
or whatever they rebrand Meta.

SCHARON HARDING, MAY 15, 2023

Double-screen "free" TV will show you ads, even when not in use

When George Orwell wrote 1984 I'm pretty sure it was as a warning against a dystopian future, and *not* as a how-to guide, however some people seem to have taken it that way, including the makers of the television reviewed in this article.

Televisions have come a long way in my lifetime, and while I greatly appreciate the larger, lighter screens and higher resolution I definitely dislike the appliance's transition from a dumb display to a "smart" surveillance device.

I could write pages on this subject, fortunately for everyone else I limited my comment to a simple couplet, with a little inspiration from Arthur C. Clarke.

TV This Century

Telly, Telly, on the wall, please tell me what to view?
"I'm sorry Dave, can't do at all – this TV watches you".

ASHLEY BELANGER, JAN 23. 2024

Patreon attacks law that keeps platforms from sharing your video views

Patreon is an online video-sharing platform that, unlike the ad-supported Youtube, allows users to store their videos behind a paywall, and charge viewers directly for access. This article reports how the company was trying to overturn an American law that prevents the sharing of a person's video viewing history.

Users of the platform had accused the company of sharing their video viewing history with Facebook by using the Meta Pixel, a piece of code that allows companies to track users' activities online.

This tracking code was already the subject of many lawsuits, and with the publication of this article it became the subject of at least one rhyme, thanks to the Ars comments.

The Meta Pixel

A little dot, a tiny square,
the smallest part of screen,
You'll never really see it,
it passes quite unseen.
And yet it's there, tagging along,
limpet-like attached,
Watching your browsing choices
with thoroughness unmatched.
A billion tiny pixels,
dragged unknowing round the net,
Shadowing our every moves
like sinister silhouettes.
Virus-like in nature,
but not spread by hacker groups,
These tiny little watchmen
are Mr Zuckerberg's shock troops.
I must admit to a morbid curiosity of sorts:
What happens when a digital speck
appears before the courts?

KYLE ORLAND, MAY 13, 2024

Game dev says contract barring "subjective negative reviews" was a mistake

The online video game storefront Steam allows developers to release their creations to the public before they are actually finished, in a scheme known as Early Access.

This allows the developers to potentially get some early revenue from their efforts, and gives fans the ability to try games early and give feedback on the game's development.

The developers of one game featuring some of Marvel's comic book characters took advantage of this feature to give away copies of an unfinished version of their game to reviewers, however anyone taking advantage of this seeming generosity had to agree to terms that prevented them from posting anything disparaging about the software.

When news of this restriction became public there was a predictable backlash, causing the developers to remove the offending terms from their conditions, however by then the damage had been done. This article on the story appeared on Ars Technica, and a comment of mine followed shortly thereafter.

Play – Nice

Sticks and stones are often thrown
(by Hawkeye and the Hulk),
But words are the most hurtful,
as they'll make a game dev sulk.
"Sure, we'll let you play our game,
you can even have it free,
But because it's Early Access
you must speak of it pleasantly".
"You cannot post unless it's nice,
or our feelings you'll offend,
Oh wait, an online backlash –
let us our terms quickly amend!"
The moral here I think is clear,
and I'm sure that you'll agree:
Games should come with *gameplay*,
and not be bound legally.

JON BRODKIN, MAY 17, 2024

Twitter URLs redirect to x.com as Musk gets closer to killing the Twitter name

After Elon Musk completed his purchase of Twitter he changed the company's name to X Corp, however it took over a year for the internet to catch up, with the X application still to be found at twitter.com during that time.

This article tells its readers how that situation has now changed, with the once-popular platform now to be found at x.com. It does a very good job of imparting this information, so I felt at least slightly justified in posting a comment that doesn't tell its readers anything nearly as useful.

Twiticide

The bird is dead! (So Elon said), now everything's an Ex!
His wives, his kids, his reputation? Yep, that all checks.
Firing half the staff was just to minimise capex,
And nothing at all to do with billionaire's complex.
But the job's not done, and our Elon's not a quitter,
So expect to hear more from your favourite heavy hitter.
After all, X is now his ego transmitter,
And he won't stop till he's flushed Twitter down the shitter.

SOCIAL

TIMOTHY B. LEE, MAR 22, 2013

Did Prenda try to intimidate ID theft victim into dropping charges?

In 2013 content creators of all sorts were still coming to grips with the Internet, as their old business models were upended by the ability of anyone to easily copy and share basically anything once it had been digitised.

One such group of content creators were studios producing "adult" content, and like many of their peers they resorted to legal methods to try and cling on to the outdated but very profitable previous status-quo.

The legal firm of choice for many of these studios was Prenda Law, who briefly became infamous for their tactics of getting a list of file-sharers from an ISP, and then sending demands for money with the threat of being taken to court for downloading porn.

Unsurprisingly most people paid up (making Prenda lots of money), and also most people despised Prenda and their tactics. The tale took an unexpected twist when it was alleged that Prenda was using someone else's identity to make legal filings, without that person's consent.

The person in question, one Alan Cooper, took Prenda to court for identity theft, prompting Prenda to file counterclaims of defamation. This article then relates how Mr Cooper then filed to have those claims dismissed as vexatious litigation.

The judge in the case, one Otis Wright, agreed that Mr Cooper had a case and ordered the Prenda principles to appear in his L.A. court.

To be honest this isn't the most interesting story Ars has ever published, but Prenda Law were generally despised by their commentariat, so the stories often had a high engagement level, if not a high news value – I suppose I can't blame Ars for running them.

I have a vague memory that there was a story on the latest Legend of Zelda game at the same time on Ars, and for reasons best left unexplored I decided to comment on the Prenda Law article using that popular game series as the premise.

The Legend of Prenda

A Hylian troll (of unknown gender),
Working as a litigation vendor,
Put file sharers through the blender,
In the name of an unwitting sender.

Now we know that this pretender,
Will soon be a first(?) offender,
But even so they won't surrender,
Though their chances will be slender,

Their ID theft did rage engender,
And the target's a contender,
Not afraid to be a spender,
And try to dent their legal fender.

When Otis his judgement does render,
They're going to need a good defender;
Maybe Link the Triforce mender?
As their asses will sure be tender.

TIMOTHY B. LEE, MAR 27, 2013

"I made some stupid posts": Anti-troll site gagged after threats against poet

This article involves both a poem and copyright, so I was always going to comment, but the details require some clarification. There is a poem called "The Dash", written by an American poet called Linda Ellis in 1996. This work is apparently a popular choice to be read at funerals, dealing as it does with life and mortality.

The poet, according to this story, is known not just for her work, but also for threatening litigation against anyone she discovers who has used The Dash without payment, such as schools, churches and funeral homes. This seems particularly heartless, and the amounts demanded were in the thousands of dollars, so not trivial.

The headline of this article relates to how the poet sought a restraining order against an anti-troll activist who had posted comments denouncing her tactics on his website. The comments apparently crossed a line, and a judge ordered that the website be shut down – a decision that other legal experts questioned.

The overall story, rather than this particular development, were what prompted my comment, and as a couple of stanzas of the poem in question were included in the story, I "borrowed" some of the first line and the structure to form my response. And against all my natural instincts I also tried to copy what I thought was the original's terrible metre and scansion.

OK, that wasn't actually that hard.

The Rash

For it matters not, if this verse rhymes,
Or whether the metre fits.
Simply by perusing these lines,
You'll soon be in the shit.

Your loved one's dead; you waved goodbye,
With verses that seemed right.
Please pay the invoice I'll supply,
All legal and polite.

After all, we've just one life,
And I really need the cash.
The problem causing me some strife
Is a nasty little rash.

CASEY JOHNSTON, SEP 3, 2013

Random access memories: My time at a singularity conference

In this story we learn how a Russian multi-millionaire named Dmitri Itskov held a conference in New York, with the aim of investigating how to make humans – particularly Mr Itskov – immortal. This would be achieved by transferring a person's consciousness into a less fragile container – a digital one to be exact.

Combined with life-like robots (presumably with eternal support contracts), this could pave the way for humanity, or at least a tiny, very rich percentage of us, to indefinitely extend our lives. If you've actually read all of the previous articles in this book you'll know that in 2013 digital piracy was also a hot topic, and the confluence of these two themes formed the basis of my comment.

Buying Time

This oligarch won't pass away –
Digitized is how he'll stay.
(And we can get clones
To run on our phones
Downloaded from the Pirate Bay).

IP would take on a whole new meaning ...

JOHN TIMMER, NOV 23, 2013

Texas school board approves all but one science text book

The United States of America, as the name might suggest, is a single country made up of many semi-autonomous regions – the states. Each state has control over what is taught in the schools within their jurisdiction, and what books are used for that teaching.

This really should not be a contentious area, however some of the more religious states take exception to science textbooks that disagree with their religious tenets, particularly in the areas of evolution and climate change.

In this article we learn how the state of Texas' school board had approved almost all of the submitted text books for use, the one exception being part-authored by someone who had testified against Creationism, when the US Congress decided that teaching that theory in schools was unconstitutional.

This pleasing news prompted me to post a comment, though I'm not sure how pleasing the comment was, particularly to fans of the classic song I ripped off to make it.

The Devil Went Down To Texas

Now the devil went down to Texas,
he was looking for a book to read,
He was feeling low as work was slow,
he was looking to spread his creed.
He came across this young man
browsing the web and typing real hard,
The devil jumped up on an office chair and said
"Son, here's my business card".

"I guess you didn't know it son,
but I'm a comment writer too",
"And if you'd care to take a dare I'll make a bet with you".
"Now you write a pretty good comment son,
but give the devil his due",
"I'll bet a keyboard of gold against your soul
'cos I think I'm better than you".
The boy said "I'm just a geezer Dev, and it might be a sin",
"But I'll take your bet, you're going to regret
'cos I'm the best there's ever been".

Geezer loosen up your keys and type your comments hard,
'Cos hell's broke loose in Texas and the devil writes on Ars.
And if you win you get this shiny keyboard made of gold –
But if you lose, the devil gets your soul!

The devil said "I'll start this show",
and pulled an iPad from his sleeve.
"I got this little gadget from a son of mine called Steve".
He ran his fingers over the screen and it made an evil hiss,
He said "I wrote the patent on unlocking things like this".
When the devil finished, Geezer said:
"Well, you're pretty good old son".

"But sit down in that chair, right there,
and let me show you how it's done".

Fire on a webpage; and here's the twist:
This geezer don't think that you exist.
Even down South they're not such fools,
To teach your crazy crap in schools.

The devil bowed his head in shame,
'cause he knew that he'd been beat,
And he laid that golden keyboard
on the ground at Geezer's feet.
Geezer said: "Just come on back
if you ever want to try again",
"'Cause I told you once, you son of a gun,
I'm the best there's ever been".

No, really, I am.

/s[7]

---

[7] At the time of writing this summary (November 2024), the Texas Board of Education has just voted to allow Bible-based lessons in public elementary schools, and the state will soon vote on whether to require the Ten Commandments to be displayed in all schools, so the optimism displayed in my comment was unfortunately misplaced.

JOE MULLIN, FEB 11, 2014

"Happy Birthday" copyright defense: Those "words" and "text" are ours

In yet another article dealing with copyright we learn how an American filmmaker is challenging the legal validity of the copyright to the song "Happy Birthday To You". The challengers allege that the melody was written in 1893 called "Good Morning To You", and the lyrics had been changed to the now common "Happy Birthday" version by the early 1900s.

It is worth noting that the owners of the copyright, the conglomerate Warner/Chappel, estimated in the 1990s that this copyright earned them more than $2 million annually. Unsurprisingly they were refuting the challengers claims, even though the copyright was originally granted in 1935, many years after the song and lyrics were written, and nearly 80 years before this litigation.

Now it just happened that at this time a video game called Portal was popular, and there were obviously some crossed wires in my brain when I commented, as features from the game got mixed up in a version of Happy Birthday, vaguely on the subject of copyright. This probably makes the poem completely inscrutable to anyone unfamiliar with all of those topics –and probably even to those who *are* familiar with them.

Profanity alert!

Totally <u>Not</u> "Happy Birthday"

An anniversary is nigh, and Glados says "Hi",
Assume the pos ... it ... ion ... (The cake is a lie).
This oval is blue, oh what can it do?
Point it at the R ... I ... A ... A, and watch them fall through.
I'll take me some grass, but on copyright I'll pass,
Those greedy motherfuckers,
can kiss my white, hairy gluteus maximus.

NATE ANDERSON, FEB 20, 2014

Science confirms: Online trolls are horrible people (also, sadists!)

This article reports how researchers in Canada published results from a study that confirmed their theories about the dominant personality traits exhibited by online trolls. These traits are narcissism, psychopathy, Machiavellianism and sadism, and they form what is known as the Dark Tetrad.

Or at least it's known to the sort of people who study these things – I'd never heard of it.

The researchers had assumed that these traits would be prevalent amongst people who enjoyed posting deliberately misleading or offensive material online, i.e. trolls. Their study confirmed these suspicions, with sadism being the predominant feature of those who confessed to such activities.

Now I don't consider myself a troll or a sadist, but this seemed like a good opportunity to put this theory to the test. Cue my comment.

Trolling, Trolling, Trolling

An honest man cannot be cheated,
(At least so I think they say).
By a placid man the troll's defeated,
If his bait is merely turned away.

Post not something you may regret,
Or get into a pointless fight, just
'Cos someone's wrong on the Internet,
And you've simply *got* to put them right.

If you're without sin then cast the first stone –
(Unless you live in a glass house),
A mote in my eye? A beam in your own!
Can you justify the views you espouse?

Argumentum ad populum and countless straw men,
Logical fallacies from astroturfers,
Appeals to pity and ad hominems,
Are not posted by the web's smartest surfers.

Enjoying your trolling? Then a sadist you are,
(And Yoda this poem did plan),
Probably born under a Narcissistic star,
Or even Machiavellian!

And if you're now thinking "at least that's not me",
"For trolling I just have no time",
Then I've got some rather bad news, you see,
You've just been trolled in rhyme :)

CATHLEEN O'GRADY, MAR 14, 2015

Is your smartphone making you dumb?

In a story reminiscent of the "calculators in the classroom" debates from my youth, this article explains how researchers set out to test whether increased smartphone use led to a decrease in analytical thinking skills.

Across a series of studies participants were asked questions to elicit both their level of reliance on smartphones, and their ability to think analytically. The results, according to the researchers, did show a correlation between a high use of technology for information retrieval and lower analytical skills.

In response to this research other scientists argued that the correlation was not causation, and it might be that less skilled thinkers would naturally be greater users of devices that helped make up for their personal weaknesses.

As a bit of a techy I personally love the idea of a pocket computer with access to much of the world's knowledge, however I'm also a curmudgeonly old fogey who loathes the unsocial[8] behaviour the gadgets cause. My comment reflected the latter of these two viewpoints.

---

[8] Yes, this is a word. Now.

Ode To CorSiritana

With phone in hand I rule the land
in winter, spring or summer,
But if it fails my brain then ails from the malady "iDumber".
In any crowd I can be proud of my social interaction –
I'll post the most and greet your tweets
with thumb-blurring reactions!
But I'm bereft when I am left with no personal assistant;
My social skills have all been killed
and my memory's not persistent.
I get my views where I get my news
(– though I think they're my opinions),
But without Yelp I'd be no help,
like all the smartphone's minions.

GLYN MOODY, AUG 3, 2015

UK peer calls for universal Internet delete button; may also want unicorns

Governments around the world have struggled with regulating the Internet for many years, and in 2015 a crossbench peer in the UK House of Lords has called for those under the age of 18 to have five "iRights", ranging from knowing who holds information on you online, to the ability to delete anything posted before your age of majority.

One of these rights would be greater digital literacy, and it probably should have been the one the peer studied *before* calling for well-intentioned but technically impossible features to be implemented by every website and online app that is accessible from the UK.

A moment's thought should be enough to realise just how infeasible this Universal Delete Button scheme is, however I have a feeling that most of the peer's thoughts were of the "think of the children" type, and not "think of the technical realities making the solution impossible" type.

The subject seemed ripe for a little poetic commentary, with a liberal dose of imagination, partly inspired by an old sci-fi TV show.

Logan's Hell

Far, far in the future, in a parallel galaxy far away where these guidelines have been in place for many years, there is a guild of facilitators tasked with preparing 18 year-olds for adult life, and this is their mantra:

Hello there son, so you've become
a man? Now heed me well!
I'll be your guide here at your side
To take you through what you must do
to thrive in Logan's Hell.

You'll quickly find that you've been blinded
by your childish dreams,
And what you've heard is all absurd
Now you can fit that adult kit
and scheme your adult schemes.

You did not know but now you'll go
through life without a net,
Now youth has flown and you have grown
You must take care to be aware
that what's said online is set.

If you must post then do not boast,
belittle or deride,
But stick to fact and try to act
As if you were right there with her
(or him) right at your side.

Your slate is clean, your past unseen,
no baggage holds you back,
So play it smart and use this start
For from this day all that you say
makes a permanent track.

A single chin and supple skin
are not what you'll miss most,
I think you'll find you've left behind
A simple thing but empowering –
a button saying "Delete Post".

This adult life is full of strife
that's recorded for all time,
Like it or not who, where and what
You do online builds a design,
even if you've done no crime.

So I'll be nice and give advice
to help you on your way,
Now what I've sown is carved in stone
I can now say the only way
to win is *not* to play.

I really should heed my own advice sometimes.

GLYN MOODY, OCT 1, 2015

Cancer patients call for UK government to override patent on £90,000-a-year drug

This article about a breast cancer drug in the UK appeared shortly after Turing Pharmaceutical, and their now infamous CEO Martin Shkreli, arbitrarily raised the price of an old anti-parasitic drug from £9 per pill to £500 per pill. As such the unaffordability of healthcare globally was in the media spotlight, and this story, first reported in the Guardian newspaper, appeared on Ars.

It relates how a group of interested parties including patients, clinicians and charities were asking the UK government to invoke a law that allowed the manufacture of patented drugs by someone other than the patent holder.

The company behind the drug in question, Roche, refused to lower the price, and this led to it being unavailable on the NHS. For-profit healthcare is a subject I could devote many stanzas to, but in this instance I restricted myself to a simple limerick.

Health. Care?

There was a greedy young business called Pharma,
Who made a drug that made everyone calmer,
But no-one could buy it,
Which then caused a riot,
And Pharma then met with his karma ...

<sigh> if only ...

BETH MOLE, NOV 7, 2020

President-elect Biden plans COVID response—while White House faces new outbreak

As the "-elect" modifier in the heading suggests, this article appeared shortly after the results of the 2020 US presidential election became known, if not universally accepted. Readers are told how the incoming winner of the election, Joe Biden, planned to deal with the ongoing Covid 19 pandemic, including keeping America in the World Health Organisation after his defeated predecessor, the 45th president, had threatened to withdraw.

As the article's comments veered a little off-topic I didn't feel *too* bad posting the following cerebral diarrhoea that impinged completely unasked upon my consciousness (with apologies to Cornershop).

Writing this summary shortly after the 2024 US election I find this rhyme a little poignant now.

45

Skinsack covered in blusher, that was 45.

Skinsack worked for Russia, that was 45.

Everybody needs a Biden for a hero, everyone needs a Biden, America needs a Biden for a hero, America needs Joe Biden; He's beaten 45.

ERIC BENDER, JUL 3, 2021

A $26-billion plan to save the Houston area from rising seas

This story, first appearing in Undark magazine, describes plans to protect the Houston coastal area from the effects of climate change, particularly sea level rise and increased storm intensity and frequency, by building a huge wall across Galveston Bay.

While most of the affected parties agreed that a solution was required, they could not all agree on what form that solution should take – or who should pay the enormous bill. As many coastal areas all faced the same challenges the demand for solutions was national, however in some of the more southerly states opposition took the form of ideological rather than financial or practical arguments.

Now there are certain locations around the world that I have never visited, but which are nevertheless seared into my consciousness thanks to a song. Examples would include Ipanema, Solsbury Hill – and Galveston. Hopefully this helps explain the form my comment took.

Galvestunned

Galveston, oh Galveston, I can see your sea is risin'!
Storms, not hope on your horizon,
Man those R's are dumb, down in Galveston.

Galveston, oh Galveston, I still hear your sea waves crashing,
Even though inland I'm dashing,
Seems my wet guns aren't much use in Galveston.

I still see her standing in the water,
Standin' there, looking at the sea,
And she is waiting there for me,
To save the beach where we used to run.

Galveston, oh Galveston, I am so afraid of drowning,
Before I watch the rednecks crowning,
A reality TV star and bum,
Oh Galveston, oh Galveston.

KIONA N. SMITH, JUL 4, 2021

Is the "Dragon Man" skull actually from a new hominin species?

When I was young – so a long time ago now, I learned that what constituted a species was the ability to produce viable offspring. Thus horses and donkeys were different species as their offspring, mules, were sterile.

However I also learned that, not only were there several "species" of humans, but that some of these species had a long history of successful interbreeding, according to our genetic record.

This article goes into some detail on these distinctions and the arguments over them amongst those in that field of research, due to the discovery of a fossilised skull that is claimed to be yet another human species.

Discovered in China, the so-called "Dragon Man" skull has features similar to both *Homo Neanderthalensis* and *Homo Denisova*, potentially placing it in a previously unseen species of hominids.

Now you may be wondering why this article is in the Social and not the Nature category – hopefully my comment will show why I thought this section was the more apt location.

Speciation By Corporation

What makes a human – is it the bones?
The DNA, protein or chromosomes?
These days we're not defined by hormones,
But more by the make of our mobile phones.

Apple man lived with his Android kin,
On the outside sharing much the same skin,
Hiding the differences to be found within,
And neither prepared to acknowledge their twin.

Are we one species, entire and whole?
Or are we more a primate casserole?
If we choose a way to each pigeonhole:
"To which corporation did you mortgage your soul?"

JOHN P. RATHBONE AND CRISTINA CRIDDLE, FEB 24, 2022

Twitter admits it mistakenly removed Ukraine open-source intelligence accounts

First published in the Financial Times, this article was obviously written *just before* Russia invaded Ukraine, and reports how Twitter, as it was then, mistakenly suspended the accounts of several users who posted open-source intelligence about the Russian military build-up.

The story was quite interesting, however by the time it was published and users were commenting the invasion had begun, and my comment reflected this updated reality, rather than staying on-topic, something you've probably already realised that I have a bit of a problem with.

I also have a problem with power-mad humans causing death and suffering to other humans on massive scales, and my comment hopefully also reflected *that* reality.

Mooting

Rootin' tootin' Putin went into Ukraine shooting,
Trying to put the boot in (and do a bit of looting).
The West tried refuting this wholesale uprooting,
Instead of parachuting in and simply executing,
Or at least prosecuting the highfalutin Rasputin,
Substituting hooting for genuine trouble-shooting,
And transmuting disputing into self-prostituting,
Thus instituting the gradual diluting
Of the freedom that I rather like.

ERIC BERGER, FEB 26, 2022

Russia pulls out of European spaceport, abandoning a planned launch

Following a few days after their invasion of Ukraine, and subsequently being sanctioned by most of the Western world, Russia announced that it would be withdrawing its personnel from the European rocket launch facility in French Guiana.

The article goes on to report that, despite some European satellites being launched from there on a modified Soyuz rocket, plans for further launches should not be affected by the Russian withdrawal.

The comments on this article quickly went off-topic, and the thread was joined by several posters writing comments supportive of the Russian position. On other forums this would have devolved into a flame war, but Ars is special; when comment threads become too out of hand there is a chance a user will post a lovely picture of some My Little Ponies, with rainbows and sparkles, and tell everyone to *just calm down*.

I found the comments rather amusing, and felt compelled to make a "meta-comment" of my own.

Off Topic

It started out as Space Talk –
but that didn't last too long,
The story involved Russia,
so some Ivans came along.
Amusingly these "tough" old Slavs
are surprisingly thin-skinned,
But peddling fascist bullshit here
is like pissing against the wind.
I'd predict a pony strike,
but actually I'm torn;
Can you chaps keep it up
'till I've finished my popcorn?

BETH MOLE, FEB 28, 2022

Majority of Ukrainian hospitals could run out of oxygen today as omicron rages: WHO

In another article following shortly after the start of the war in Ukraine, readers are told how the unprovoked invasion has affected the supply of medical oxygen to Ukrainian hospitals, threatening the lives of patients suffering from severe Covid.

There have been humans at war with other humans for every day of my life, but I've been extremely fortunate that those wars were all far away – until Mad Vlad tried to grab a chunk of eastern Europe.

I'm not really the most cheerful chap at the best of times, and the needless suffering filling the media daily – including my favourite science website, caused my outlook to become even more than usually depressed.

Hopefully that explains – if not excuses, my rather dark, and as usual off-topic comment.

So Said The Crow

"Here we go again" said the crow (again),
"even though they'd said 'never more!'"
"The dumb, bald monkeys are at it again,
playing the game they call war".
"While most just want to get on with their lives,
with wives, and children and such",
"For'a select few this just will not do,
and for them there's never too much".
"You'd think that the rest would realise what's best
and get rid of all of those fools",
"However, instead they give them their bread,
and let them make all of the rules!"
"They rip out the trees and displace the bees
that they need for the food that they eat",
"Don't they realise that without compromise
they'll soon become – obsolete?"
"But while it lasts and until it's past I'll head East,"
(as the crow flies),
"We Corvids aren't dumb, I'mma go get me some
of those tasty dumb monkey eyes".

BETH MOLE, MAR 24, 2022

Ex-Goop exec decries "toxic" wellness culture—while promoting a cleanse

For readers (or listeners) unfamiliar with Goop, they are a company founded by the actor Gwyneth Paltrow, that sells "wellness" products, perhaps most famously some chunks of "special" rock that allegedly provide "wellness" when inserted into a bodily orifice.

Other so-called wellness products include items to remove things from other orifices, involving purges and cleanses and other mediaeval pseudo-medicine, so I suppose it balances out in the end. Pun unapologetically intended.

The "wellness" sector is sort of like the health sector, but critically it is not governed by the finicky regulations that apply to health products, little things like testing for efficacy and non-toxicity or lethality. Companies in the sector try to position themselves as "premium" brands, because if you're going to sell snake oil to idiots you might as well sell expensive snake oil to rich idiots.

This article, by the wonderful Beth Mole, does a far better job than I could of describing how Elise Loehnen, an ex-executive from Goop, complained that the culture at that company was "toxic", and that she'd changed her "distorted" views on her health and diet, all whilst promoting similar products from an alternative brand of "wellness" purveyors.

My comment was nowhere near as cleverly snarky as Beth's article – but my take on the story *sort of* rhymes, so there's that.

Anatomical colloquialisms ahead.

Excellent Excrement

When you need to poop is when you need Goop,
(but only if you've got class).
Just take this Gooper Super Pooper Scooper
And stick it up your arse.
Made from the horn of a unicorn,
Just poke it between your legs.
And if there's no space in that private place
First remove those vaginal eggs.
Don't think of it as shovelling shit,
Or your wellness you may sap.
For when your colon's clear, with no smear to the rear
Replace your faeces with some of *our* crap.

JAMES M. SMOLIGA, DVM, PhD, NOV 10, 2023

Is the NFL making progress in tackling its concussion crisis?

The NFL was one of the first sports to investigate the potentially long term injurious effects of participating in their pastime, specifically whether there was any link between repeated concussions while playing football, and high incidences of mental disorders in retired players.

Other sports, including soccer and rugby in the UK, are also now looking into how they can do a better job of making their professional occupations safer. This article, written by an expert on the subject, gives a detailed and informed account of the state of these NFL investigations, and the steps that they are taking to try and make their games a little safer.

As someone who follows what is called in my country "American Football" I'm pleased that the league is taking these steps, however the cynic in me thinks this is more due to the potential multi-billion dollar legal liability they might face if they don't, rather than any actual consideration for the welfare of the players. It was this cynical side of my nature that wrote my comment.

Third And Ten

Under centre I call the snap, the O-line springs as one,
I just have time to think "Oh crap" when I'm hit by half a ton
Of D-line and a safety blitz, I mustn't lose the ball!
But my body is reduced to bits, and I pass out as I fall ...

The smelling salts bring me round, just where the heck am I?
"Easy son – stay on the ground. You'll be just fine, tough guy".
"We had to punt, then got a stop –
 there's time for one last drive",
"Just one TD and we'll reach the top –
(assuming you survive)".

JENNIFER OUELLETTE, DEC 20, 2023

Great British Bake Off's festive Christmas desserts aren't so naughty after all

I have to confess that I am not really a huge fan of cookery programmes; my fussy palate envies those who can apparently stuff almost anything into their mouths and enjoy it, but as I'd find many of the delicious-to-others recipes completely inedible my viewing tastes tend elsewhere.

I am however aware of the cultural phenomena that is the Great British Bake Off, so when this article appeared on Ars I at least had some clue what it was about.

To give you a hint of its flavour, the meat of the story relates how researchers studied some of the dessert recipes used on the show, and found that, possibly contrary to expectations, some of them included healthy ingredients.

This is certainly food for thought, and without making too much of a meal of it my comment tried to commemorate these rather appetising findings.

G.B.B.O G.O.O.D

The set is the kitchen they're stood in,
The implements metal and wooden,
The task is to bake
An unhealthy cake,
But it turned out the puddin' had good in.

CYRUS FARIVAR, JUN 21, 2012

The Internet's most hated man

The Internet of 2012 seems like a very young and rather naive place compared to the web of today, however this article from that year could probably have been published at any time, dealing as it does more with human egos than technology.

The article relates how the attorney for a website called FunnyJunk, one Charles Carreon, had been so incensed by what he considered defamatory comments by the author of the webcomic The Oatmeal that he sent a cease and desist letter demanding $20,000.

The owner of The Oatmeal responded to this attempted extortion by replying with a picture of a mother having sex with a bear, and then started a fundraiser to get the $20,000. Not to pay Mr Carreon, but to send him a picture of the money before giving it to various charities.

Mr Carreon, who claims to represent "the good and the good-looking", was even less impressed with this reply, and responded by personally suing or threatening to subpoena basically everyone – the owner of the Oatmeal, the charities, the fund-raising site, someone who had impersonated him on Twitter, Twitter, and Ars Technica where the impersonator had owned up to their deeds.

The Internet disapproved of this attempted litigation, and the hapless lawyer found himself the recipient of unwanted pizza deliveries, porn site subscriptions and just general hate mail. Also some particularly bad poetry, so take that, Charles!

Irksome Jerks

Heroes of the poor appear in most cultures;
England had Robin Hood and Maid Marian.
In the US the internet vultures
Are amusing themselves by eating (chuck) carrion...

With his tinted John Lennons and trendy t-shirt,
He defends the unwilling from his outer space station.
The good and good looking will never be hurt,
With Charlie to shield them from defamation.

Just don't mention his mother – or Kodiak bears,
Lest his Disney-esque wrath be unleash'd 'pon the net.
An atomic reaction that will draw more than stares,
(Pizzas, subscriptions and porn pics, I'd bet).

ERIC BANGEMAN, JUN 30, 2012

Limerweek in review: the week's top news in rhyme

I am far from the only amateur poet in the world, and in this article from 2012 it transpired that Ars Technica harboured another budding bard.

As the title suggests this article wasn't a science story as such, but rather an attempt to turn some of the stories published during the previous week into some form of poetry. There weren't many comments, and there were even fewer positive ones; humans tend to forget that we're the worst poets in the entire Galaxy – the Vogons were only the third worst.

Feeling that the article had set the bar rather low I felt confident enough to throw my metaphorical hat into the comment ring, along with another commenter going by yesnomaybe. Also the two stories I chose to versify had already been subjects of my artistic aspirations (see previous rhyme), so I had a bit of a head start.

Poetry *Isn't* Easy

Ars poetica this ain't,
like yesnomaybe I hate your scansion,
The rhymes are forced and the metre faint.
Hide this verse in Kim Dotcom's mansion.
(It should be safe, the raid weren't legal –
Team America fell off their eagle).
And to the legal rampage,
by Arizona's wayward son –
Your wife Godwinned your webpage –
but please Charles, carry on!

KEN FISHER, OCT 4, 2012

Introducing comment voting on news articles and features

Websites such as Ars Technica that have existed for much or all of the Internet's brief history have had to evolve as the technology that powers the World Wide Web has advanced.

This article introduced a new feature to my favourite science website, namely the ability for readers to express their opinion of others' comments by either up- or down-voting them.

As a sensitive artiste (note the trailing "e"), I found this news potentially alarming; comments with significant downvotes would be hidden in the thread, and I feared that my off-topic ramblings would likely fall foul of this so-called upgrade.

I also tend to suffer from significant cynicism, and thought that there was an unmentioned aspect to the new feature that might have indicated an ulterior motive to its introduction, as I noted in my comment.

Hating Comment Rating

Alas for Ars, and woe is me!
They've metered creativity!

For comments on here now can be
downvoted to obscurity!
As if "Ignore" was not enough
for others who don't like my stuff,
I won't just face their rant and puff –
I'll have a vote count to rebuff.
Unless, of course – could it be true –
is there appreciation too?
Doh – I'll get whatever's due
(likely a judicial review).
Now if page hits are your desire,
then this feature could light your fire:
"I'll just check if my votes are dire –
or possibly they've gotten higher ..."
A user feature to be sure –
and also just a little more –
Page impressions come galore
when everyone's checking their score.
But don't mind me and my dissent –
I might just be ambivalent;
Just don't expect me to relent –
my rhymes do not need your consent!

SEBASTIAN ANTHONY, MAY 5, 2015

Welcome to Ars Technica UK!

For a brief period in the history of Ars Technica the website featured a UK-focused section, and this article introduced it and the authors to Ars' readers.

While this initiative was ultimately unsuccessful I did celebrate its launch with what I hoped was a welcoming comment.

Ars Britannia

It's jolly good to meet you chaps
(and the new chapette too),
One might hope that now perhaps
we'll hear a Blighty view.
Exchange your POTUS for our PM, NSA for GCHQ.
Actually, on second thoughts that might be nothing new.

It's a bit too late to get irate
over our Americanization,
It's not so great as the 51st state
when you thought you were a nation.
Well anyway, all things UK, like big red double-deckers,
Are very good but what I would like's a UK spell-checker!

Where "data" rhymes with "hater", and colour has a "u",
And if you say "aloominum" everyone laughs at you,
Just so long as you don't go wrong
and forget about the science,
Or I'll waste time writing crappy rhymes
to signal my defiance!

PUBLIC COMMENT THREAD, OCT 6, 2015

LG ad subverting "dark on light" format for home page.

Unlike the other comments in this book that were posted in response to an actual story on Ars Technica, this comment was made on the site's public forums, where a topic had sprung up discussing an advert recently appearing on the site's home page.

The advert was far more technical than a simple graphic, presumably to impress the presumably technical readers of Ars. Featuring mouse-tracking technology a light-source in the advert would follow a user's cursor around the page, making it very eye-catching.

This also made it very intrusive and annoying, and the code for the advert somehow interfered with the website's user preferences for which theme to use, a bug that irked many commenters.

It also irked me, but unlike the other more mature posters I expressed my displeasure in something approximating rhyme, taking another old Billy Joel song as my inspiration. Note that Ars is owned by the publisher Condé Nast.

Condé Nasty

"What's the matter with the ads you're getting?"

"Can't you tell that they're total shite?"

"Maybe we should let them change our user's settings?"

"If you do you'll be in for a fight ..."

"Don't you know this is 2015, honey",

"We're not here for readers, we're here to make money";

"Hot punk, cool funk, even if it's old junk"

"It's money in the bank for Condé".

KIONA N. SMITH, JUL 13, 2021

A Neanderthal carved a geometric design in bone 51,000 years ago

In the Harz Mountains of northern Germany there is a cave, and a very long time ago (by human standards), some very old humans lived there, eating the local fauna – cave lions, bears, bison and giant deer.

They probably also ate the local flora, but, unlike the animals, the plants didn't leave behind any bones. One of these left-behind bones was the second toe bone of a giant deer, and it had been carved with geometric patterns by one of these very old humans.

Carving patterns into things is something that newer humans like to think is unique to them, so this finding was of scientific interest, as Homo Sapiens hadn't arrived in the area at the time the bone was carved, ruling out any artistic influences from our own strain of hominids.

Researchers tried to duplicate the markings using contemporaneous tools and found that it would require about 20 flint blades and 1 ½ hours work to create – so not a trivial or spur-of-the-moment undertaking.

For a long time I've been impressed with early humans' ability to not just survive but thrive in what must have been a very challenging environment, and I could have made that the basis of my comment; instead I sank to the level of some of the previous posters in speculating on the purpose of the artefact, noting its vaguely phallic shape.

Neolithic Prick

Ug the caveman had a bone;
he rubbed it with a rock,
He rubbed that bone with many stones,
until he had – a cock?

DIANA GITIG, JUL 31, 2021

World Brain: Wells, Welles, Orwell, and the role of information in society

H. G. Wells is probably best known as the author of several famous works of early science fiction, however in his later life he travelled the world giving a series of lectures on subjects dear to his heart. This article informs its readers of the re-release of a compendium of these lectures, and considers how the world has changed since they were first given.

That was in 1938-9, just before the start of the Second World War; during the first war Wells had been appointed the British Director of Enemy Propaganda Against Germany, and the views he espoused at his lectures were coloured by his experiences and thinking at that time.

Which was slightly ironic, given that the thrust of the lectures was to argue for humanity to think differently so as not to repeat the mistakes of the past, using a cumulative store of mankind's knowledge as a unifying World Brain.

He proposed that, if everyone were given the same education and access to knowledge, and abandoned their nationalistic tendencies, then global peace and understanding would naturally ensue.

A few years later another noted author George Orwell published a piece entitled "Wells, Hitler and the World State" in which he noted that Nazi Germany was closer to the groupthink utopia proposed by his near-contemporary, but was run by a criminal lunatic, so didn't actually lead to harmony and prosperity.

As this article notes, with the Internet and mobile phones most humans now have a World Brain at their fingertips, and neither of the famous author's predictions had been proved completely correct.

I do not consider myself in the company of such greats of literature, but I do have ideas on the perfidies of human nature, and I wasn't too bashful to post them as my comment.

The Human Lament
(I Don't Believe in Adam and Eve)

I had a dream of a lovely world,
a world of peace and love,
A world where no insult is hurled,
and push won't turn to shove.
A place where man helps fellow man, regardless of his tribe,
He helps him just because he can, requiring no bribe.

CHORUS
Oh people, how did we come this far?
I don't believe in Adam and Eve, who do we think we are?

A good deed is its own reward, at least in my dream land,
Where not one person is ignored who needs a helping hand.
Where all are equal 'neath the sun, with recourse to the law,
Where one for all and all for one, and none has less or more.

I'm not the first to have this dream, I may not be the last,
I dream despite what I have seen,
from the lessons of the past.
I dream for those who're yet to come,
and hope that they will see,
The world I dream of could become,
if everyone thought like me!

Coda

And thus the problem is laid bare, the cause of our distress,
It's not enough to just declare "My viewpoint is the best".
You can be right; you can be true; you do not need to lie,
And still I'll disagree with you, and here's the reason why:

My life is mine; like DNA each one is quite unique,
And so with sadness I must say the "greater truth" we seek,
May never to humans belong,
and though the thought may sting,
We cherish the right to be *wrong* – it's a very human thing.

SCOTT K. JOHNSON, AUG 6, 2021

A look back at (very bad) predictions of global cooling

According to this article from 2021, both climate science and anti-climate science had been around long enough for the predictions they made to be compared to reality, and only one of these two sets of projections was correlated with the observed facts.

Comprising a list of forecasts about the climate that tried to deny a warming trend caused by human activity, and comparing them to the actual observed situation, the story probably wouldn't make happy reading for climate change deniers. I have a feeling they wouldn't enjoy the reality-based science reporting on Ars Technica generally, so hardly a cause for concern.

The line from the piece that caught my attention wasn't actually climate-change related; the author said of those who had made the now-proved-wrong predictions "Like the cringeworthy poetry you wrote in high school, they probably hope that everyone will just forget about it.".

As you're reading (or listening) to this book you'll know that not *everyone* stopped in high school, as I think I ably demonstrated with my comment.

Cringeworthy

You may ask whether we'll weather this weather,
and all I can say is "we'll try, mate".
I'll just take my pliers to all these deniers
and see how they like *that* climate.

JOHN TIMMER, AUG 9, 2021

Court rules Florida-based cruise lines can ask for vaccine certification

In America the response to the Covid pandemic was complicated by the patchwork nature of that country, with federal and state laws often in conflict. If one were to make a study of these conflicts a pattern might become apparent – namely that the states passing laws contrary to federal health advice were generally controlled by Republican legislators.

This article highlights one such example in the state of Florida, which had passed a law prohibiting any business from requiring proof of Covid vaccination before providing their services. Norwegian Cruise Line Holdings, a company that ran several ships from ports in Florida had however offered a cruise where everyone on board had to provide proof of being vaccinated, following CDC guidelines and as required by several locations the cruises would visit.

The company sued the state and obtained a preliminary injunction, on the grounds that the Florida law was likely to be found unconstitutional. In a rare exception to my normal routine of just making up some poorly rhyming rubbish and posting it as quickly as possible, I had recently written a few verses of poorly rhyming and rather rude rubbish that was on a vaguely related subject, and I posted that instead. I doubt anyone noticed the difference.

The Ballad of Redneck Joe

Now this is the tale of Redneck Joe,
an all-American good ole boy,
Born on the farm where pappy Joe was born
(sort of like a Joe convoy).
His mother's and his sister's name
was Mary-Bobby-Sue;
She had begun while still quite young
like girls in those parts do.

Now once a month his pappy would leave,
driving off to the nearest town,
Where he'd buy supplies from the usual guys,
before chucking a couple down.
When he'd drunk his fill of the local swill
he'd then be on his way,
And he'd tell his son of all the fun in Crapsville, USA.

Now there came a time when pappy was sick,
and Joe thought he was stuck,
But pappy said "You're a grown man now,
so you can take the truck".
"Just turn this key, and move this knob,

push this to go and that to stop,
Take the key out to turn it off,
now off you go and save our crop!"

So clutching tightly to the wheel
Joe lurched and shuddered down the road,
Until he got a puncture and he
found his progress somewhat slowed.
But then came a man in an old blue car,
and he saw our hero's plight,
Though he simply couldn't stop himself
from laughing at the sight.

"Hey there, son" he called to Joe, "are you a total twat?"
"Why don't you pull over up there
and let me take a look at that?"
But Joe was proud and didn't like
strangers calling him names,
So just for fun he pulled his gun and said "Let's test my aim".

As you'd surmise it's no surprise
that the man in the blue car fled,
But before too long another came along,
only this one was new and red.
Now when this chap saw Joe he thought
"I've got a right one here",
And all the while hiding his smile he pulled up really near.

"Hey there, son" he called across, "You seem a solid man",
"Through and through you're truest blue,
under that manly tan".
"I see you have an issue here, but today's your lucky day,"
"For though this is a lonely road
an expert has come your way!"

Now Joe liked this man very much, despite his perfumed hair,
(And his manicured fingernails, and his slightly pompous air).
So with a smile he stopped the truck
and said "Let's make a deal,
I haven't got much money but I need to fix my wheel".

Now Don (the chap in the red car) said
"Son, that sounds right fine!"
"I knew you were a Christian man with values just like mine!"
"You've only got one hundred bucks?
Well then, I'll tell you what",
"Though it's but half my usual fee, I'll take what you have got".

"Now your problem is this wheel right here,
as I'm sure that you can see",
"The problem being that it doesn't match,
doesn't match with the other three".
"But don't you fret – I am the best, I have a special trick",

"I'm going to poke the other wheels
with this here pointy stick".

"There you go, now all four match! I know that you'll go far!"
"Now tell me son, did you happen to see
a man in an old blue car?"
"Why yes" said Joe, "he called me names.
I really didn't like him",
"And just for fun I pulled my gun –
but I didn't really strike him".

"Them's lousy librul commies, son" said Don. "You be aware",
"They hate you and the USA – but I've got you in my care!"
"You want to really show them
that you're going to take a stand?"
"The one thing they hate most of all is if I relieve my glands".

"So show them you're a real man who will let no insult pass",
"Just turn around and bend on over
and let me fuck your arse".
"Ah, yes, that's great! We really showed
those socialists who's boss!"
"(*And* I'll just remind you that I helped you at a loss)".

And from that day Joe's path was set –
and I'll just add this note:
Read 'tween the lines, there's a parable
about the colour of your vote.

BETH MOLE, AUG 10, 2021

Florida is ablaze with COVID-19—and its case data reporting is a hot mess

Following a day after the previous article dealing with the Floridian response to the Covid pandemic, this article informs its readers how the state has both terrible case numbers and also terrible case number reporting.

Serving as yet another example of politically motivated meddling in public health matters, the story should make sobering reading to anyone, not just residents of the USA. As a resident of the UK, where we had the misfortune of having the least competent PM[9] in recent memory at the helm at the time of this national emergency, I felt I should try and give some moral support to my American cousins by noting in my comment that the virus was global.

On reflection that probably isn't actually a comforting thought, but, like the previous comment I had some almost relevant material ready to go, and this innocent thread was where I chose to post it.

---

[9] I'd forgotten Liz Truss – but then I don't have a mortgage.

The UK CoronaVirus Blues

```
C                            F
```
I can still remember when I heard it on the news,
```
C                                  F
```
The story I'd been waiting for, but not one that I'd choose,
```
Am                         Em
```
The doom we'd been foretelling of the people that we'd lose,
```
C         F       G7            C
```
And since then I've been suffering the coronavirus blues.

CHORUS (REPEAT BETWEEN EACH VERSE)
```
F                  Am
```
Covid n-n-nineteen, and Sars-Cov-2,
```
F                   G
```
Invisible invaders trying to kill me and you,
```
F                  Am
```
Clever little buggers, to give them their due,
```
   C      F       G7       C
```
But is it any wonder that I'm feeling blue?

So it started out in China, and then spread to Italy,
(Well, it started out in bats, at least allegedly),
And then it came to Europe, to visit you and me,
And despite all the warnings, we still weren't ready.

Now I try to be forgiving but some things I can't excuse,
Like those whose job in life it was to pick up on these cues,

They weren't aware, they showed no care,
they must have had a snooze,
And since then I've been suffering the coronavirus blues.

Care homes were the first to go, the frail and elderly,
Hospitals had no O_2, and none had PPE,
But a bunch of Tory donors became even more wealthy,
The old were dying in their homes,
but they drank their Chablis.

Who'd have thought we would feel bad
for those upon a cruise?
Looking back, would anyone want
to have been in their shoes?
Shunned like old-time lepers in their luxury canoes,
And since then I've been suffering the coronavirus blues.

We had no drugs, we had no hope,
a lockdown was decreed,
And at the local superstore this caused a great stampede,
"Forget the food, forget the drink –
it's bog rolls that we need!"
I ask you who would not feel blue at such a show of greed?

I suppose I shouldn't be surprised; isn't one of our taboos,
Getting caught a wee bit short in need of number twos,

And finding out that we're without the requisite tissues?
And since then I've been suffering the coronavirus blues.

And so we hid ourselves away
(and grew some great hair-dos),
No-one got their nails done, and no-one got tattoos,
Pubs and restaurants had to close,
or converted to drive-thrus,
And since then I've been suffering the coronavirus blues.

Any who were drinkers got stuck right in to the booze,
What else were we supposed to do
while waiting for breakthroughs?
And watching through a face-palm
as our leaders made miscues,
And since then I've been suffering the coronavirus blues.

Down every road, down every lane, down all the avenues,
We bunkered down like in the war, but in our ones and twos,
As chaps we'd never seen before gave daily interviews,
And since then I've been suffering the coronavirus blues.

Life was tough for those who had some children to amuse,
But not as hard as those who were
locked in with their abuse,
For some human behaviour there really is no good excuse,
And since then I've been suffering the coronavirus blues.

Before too long the pressure grew
and loose came many screws,
People were a tinder box – and Covid was the fuse,
Even sleepy Bristol tore down all of their statues,
And since then I've been suffering the coronavirus blues.

Epidemiology became a word we'd often see,
With graphs and charts and statistics
all over our primetime TV,
Instead of real audiences and live interviewees,
As talking heads sat on their beds and broadcast remotely.

From kid to gran we all began to become webcam gurus,
No sports events were taking place;
for once the bookies lose,
And now we all stand far apart whenever we're in queues,
And that's why I've been suffering the coronavirus blues.

From Birmingham to Bangalore, from Rome to Santa Cruz,
From Wisconsin to Wichita, New York to Syracuse,
From the rolling plains of Africa home to those proud Zulus,
Up to the Arctic circle where they live in those igloos,
Even the land down under which we share with kangaroos,
Christians, Muslims, Humanists, Taoists, atheists, Jews,
Quakers, Amish, Pentecostal, Born again, Hindus,
Covid really doesn't care which of us it pursues,

So we wash our hands, we wear our masks
and mind our p's and q's,
And that's why I've been suffering.
And that's why I've been suffering,
And that's why I've been suffering the Corona. Virus. Blues![10]

---

[10] The chords and tab for this song and a few others can be found at ultimate-guitar.com – search for justageezer.

ERIC BANGEMAN, DEC 24, 2021

The 20 most-read stories of 2021 on Ars Technica

A helpfully self-explanatory heading should render any further explication of the article itself unnecessary, and continuing a trend I posted a pre-prepared piece as my comment. My intent was to show my gratitude to the Ars staff for enriching my life – my execution may have been lacking.

Arscape (Not The Pina Coladas Song)

(But if you can talk a friend or colleague into going "Ba-boom, boom, boom!" after every line or comma, then you're more persuasive than I am. Or, you know, you just *have* friends or colleagues. Anyway ...)

I was tired of my news feed. (This is ten years ago).
I needed better content, from the people in the know.
So while everyone was sleeping, I went searching around.
And after many false starts, here's the website I found:

"You'll like reading Ars Technica, if you have half a brain,
If you're interested in science, then please let us explain.

If you like making stuff at midnight, or collect figurines,
Find the viewpoints you've looked for,
we know what everything means!"

[Solo break – air synth / air sax]

I didn't think about my sports sites, I was tired of that scene.
I wanted something stimulating (but that wasn't obscene).
So I bookmarked that website, and set up my account.
I would have bought a subscription, but I lacked that amount.

If you like reading Ars Technica, then please let me explain:
I know that you're into science,
and that you have half a brain.
You must like making things from Lego,
or just fiddling with stuff.
And as long as it's not children, well then that's good enough.

[Solo break – air spoons / air clapping]

So I've been reading with interest, and it's been a right lark.
What with tactical ponies, and Ed-it-or Moonshark.
I've been out there with Berger, on the fringes of space,
And if Kyle plays Forza, I'd like to give him a race.

I'm far dimmer than Timmer, and less punny than Mole,
(And I'd better mention Aurich, lest he swallow me whole).
And all the others I like reading too, there's too many to list.

204

I'm sure you'd all like a shout-out(!),
and I hope you're not pissed.

But my favourites are the physics ones, written by Mr. Lee,
Even though I only understand, about one word in three.
(But he needs to change his photograph,
and wear a different coloured Tee.
As he looks like a felon, in the penitentiary).

[Final solo break – air shaker played at waist level]

So I like reading Ars Technica, though I've but half a brain.
And I'm really into science, though I find it a strain.
I'd like making stuff from Lego, But that's something I lack,
Instead I write crappy poetry, and I'm afraid I'll be back.

Ba-boom, boom, Boom!

[drop mic, knock over guitar, pick up guitar, exit stage right]
[bump into wall, try to look cool, exit stage left]
[bump into another fucking wall, fail to look cool (again), exit stage front, to shower of effusive praise (in the form of beer bottles)]

DIANA GITIG, DEC 31, 2021

Animals vs. humans vs. machines: who's got smarts?

In this, the second book review article to feature in this compilation, readers are given an overview of a book titled "Bots and Beasts" that asks – and consequently tries to answer, the question "What makes machines, animals and people smart?".

The author, Paul Thagard, is a philosopher and cognitive scientist who has written extensively on similar topics, so I'm sure the arguments were well informed and well expressed, however as with the first book review I found the subject interesting, but not sufficiently compelling to inspire a purchase.

Also, I had my own ideas on the subject, which, whilst far less informed or well expressed, had, in my opinion, the significant advantage of almost rhyming.

Clever /= Wise

Humans can be stupid and charmless,
Even more than creatures that're armless,
We've mastered the dumbs,
Despite opposable thumbs.
Just smart enough to be *mostly* harmless.

BENJ EDWARDS, 21 AUG, 2024

Ars Technica content is now available in OpenAI services

Reporting Ars Technica's parent company, Condé Nast, had signed an agreement with OpenAI, a prominent player in the LLM arena, this article prompted me to post my final rhyming comment, so I'd guess that Ars probably wish they'd made the deal much earlier.

An argument presented in favour of the deal was basically "they were scraping the data before, now we're at least getting paid for it", which I have some sympathy for. I appreciate the work the writers at Ars do, and A.I. threatens them far more than it does me, despite the site's current stance of not posting anything directly A.I. generated.

Sadly the data being scraped includes not just the articles but also any comments – that includes everything in this book. Had I been able to predict this scenario ten years ago I might have deliberately posted even more nonsensical rubbish in order to pollute the A.I. datasets more than I actually did, but as there are plenty of others unselfconsciously doing that anyway I probably shouldn't worry.

We all should.

Web of Lies

In far off days (and a purple haze),
the tech bros hatched a plan:
To store on networked PCs all the knowledge gained by man.
Accessible to everyone – a place for all to come;
Unfortunately they forgot that most of us are dumb.

When all can publish equally, regardless of their sanity,
The end result, I think you'll see, is not a place of harmony.
With wannabes chasing celebrity
with hyperbole and conspiracy,
You get a toxic potpourri that doesn't match reality.

And then the cherry on the cake,
to multiply this great mistake,
This mess of lies with truth opaque,
is hoovered up as the intake
Of programs made by some of us,
that make the rest superfluous –
No wonder it's caused such a fuss –
feel free to cuss while you discuss!

Note that you can easily tell an original justageezer rhyme because it's nowhere near as good as the OpenAI ones. 100% original human rubbish.

Closing Thoughts

Firstly let me say that, if you *have* actually read (or listened to) every word I've written on your way to this paragraph, my heartiest thanks and congratulations to you, gentle reader. I believe there are some excellent services available to help with your PTSD (Post The-Ars-Skives Stress Disorder).

And if you skipped to this bit well, I don't blame you, and you'll be glad to hear that this is likely the only book of this kind I'll write and compile, as anything now posted to Ars gets fed into an A.I. for future mangled regurgitation. Which you'd know if you'd read the whole book.

While the work herein was gladly posted online and accessible to all for free, and I am lucky enough not to have to rely on my creative skills for a living (because, let's face it, I'd be screwed), I still resent mega-corps using their resources to hoover up as much of the Internet as possible, for their sole future profit, and at the expense of and without the permission of the creators of that content.

My youthful, utopian vision of automation, robotics and artificial intelligence freeing humanity to spend their time doing science, art and other leisure activities, has been distorted into a dystopian reality where those very technologies my naive self so desired are now warped by the insatiable lust for power and wealth of a few of us into the very tools of our oppression. Or something.

But that's a rather down-beat tone to end the book, so please don't mind me, but enjoy your brief moment alive in this astonishing universe, and know that its story will continue long after our tiny chapter in it is finished.

And if you did skip to the end it's as you thought – the butler did it.

Dedication

To my family generally and my wonderful mother specifically – thanks for everything, and sorry, but you *are* related to me.

– Respect Existence, or Expect Resistance[11] –

© justageezer 2024. justageezer@hotmail.com

---

[11] I wish I'd come up with this.

Printed in Great Britain
by Amazon

9965d0aa-4440-4f5a-bae2-776ffe894ad0R01